*From the notoriously slippery ("It depe
is is."—President Bill Clinton) to the geogra
be here in the great state of Chicago."—Dar.*

of the stupidest things ever said by the men and women we've elected to lead us.

The Stupidest Things Ever Said By Politicians

"If you take out the killings, Washington actually has a very low crime rate."
—Marion Barry, mayor of Washington, D.C.

"We've got a strong candidate. I'm trying to think of his name."
*—Senator Christopher Dodd,
Democratic National
Committee cochairman*

"People don't want handouts! People want hand jobs!"
*—Connecticut governor William O'Neill at a 1998 political rally
(His comment was followed by riotous applause.)*

"I always wait until a jury has spoken before I anticipate what they will do."
—U.S. Attorney General Janet Reno

"Who are these guys?"
*—Vice President Al Gore referring to the busts of Jefferson, Washington,
Franklin, and the Marquis de Lafayette on a televised tour of Monti-
cello, home of Thomas Jefferson, as CNN cameras rolled*

Other books by Ross and Kathryn Petras

The 776 Stupidest Things Ever Said
The 776 Even Stupider Things Ever Said
The 776 Nastiest Things Ever Said
The 776 Stupidest Things Ever Done
Very Bad Poetry
Stupid Sex
Stupid Celebrities
Stupid Movie Lines
The 365 Stupidest Things Ever Said Annual Calendar

The
Stupidest
Things Ever
Said By
Politicians

Ross and Kathryn Petras

POCKET BOOKS

NEW YORK LONDON TORONTO SYDNEY TOKYO SINGAPORE

An *Original* Publication of POCKET BOOKS

 POCKET BOOKS, a division of Simon & Schuster Inc.
1230 Avenue of the Americas, New York, NY 10020

ISBN: 0-671-04053-7

First Pocket Books trade paperback printing September 1999

10 9 8 7 6 5 4 3 2 1

POCKET and colophon are registered trademarks of Simon & Schuster Inc.

*Cover design by Rod Hernandez; front cover illustration by Dan Shefelman
Book design by Nancy Singer Olaguera*

Printed in the U.S.A.

RRDHC/✕

ACKNOWLEDGMENTS

Thanks, as always, to our wonderful agent, Kris Dahl; her superb assistant, Sean Desmond; and our truly fabulous editor, Kim Kanner.

And a special thanks to the intrepid souls who—with keen ears and eyes, as well as a well-developed sense of the absurd—found and submitted gems of stupidity that are included in this book:

Ada and Andre Barcinski
Isaac Bernstein
Jonathan Brecht
Marianne Cone
Ally Cunningham
Paul Denhup
Joel Eisenberg
Margaret and Joel Harris
Brian Kelly
Paul Kroenhke
Jan and Chris Lovegren
Tanya Maes
Robert Moser
Carl McManus

Clair Schwan
Parker and Jamie Taylor
Angela Vitale
Sam Wheeler
Mike Yohe

—and all the others who wish to remain anonymous. . . . Keep 'em coming!

INTRODUCTION

Reader, suppose you were an
idiot, and suppose you were a
member of Congress. But I
repeat myself.
—*Mark Twain*

A fine statement, to be sure—and one with which many would wholeheartedly agree. However, we must take exception (to some degree) to Mr. Twain's pithy words. In total candor, not all members of Congress are idiots. And, to extend the point, not all *politicians* are idiots. But virtually all, at one point or another, say something idiotic that does give one pause.

Thus this book, *The Stupidest Things Ever Said By Politicians.*

Yes, there are those times—occasionally—when our politicians say intelligent things, or at least intelligible things. But in this book we've chosen to exercise our editorial prerogative and focus solely on their stupidest, dumbest, most inane utterances.

And why not? We pay for our politicians, bureaucrats, and leaders—we pay their salaries, we pay for their perks, we pay for their retirements. Why not a laugh or two at their expense?

So we've collected over seven hundred of the stupidest things politicians, bureaucrats, and others affiliated with government have ever said. We've focused on recent stupidity, but to prove that political stupidity knows no age, we have included the most egregiously stupid political quotes from the past. We've also tried to be as nonpartisan as possible in everything, because humor knows no party or ideology. Stupidity is, after all, the most democratic (with a small *d*) of human traits.

We'd Like to Hear from You . . .

We are always eager to hear from fellow aficionados of stupid quotes. If you've heard, read, or somehow sensed a particularly good stupidity from a politician or government official, feel free to E-mail us at **stupidest@aol.com** or write to us in care of our publisher:

Ross and Kathryn Petras
c/o Pocket Books
1230 Avenue of the Americas
New York, New York 10020

Please provide us with a source for your quotation, and let us know if you'd like to be credited in print if we use it in a forthcoming book or in our annual calendar, The 365 Stupidest Things Ever Said.

The
Stupidest
Things Ever
Said By
Politicians

On Advice, Not All That Helpful

Well, I don't know. I thought I did well—but then maybe I didn't. So I don't know. I leave it up to the senator here. He's got it figured out. I can't divulge it, though. I feel good about it, I really do.

George Bush when asked what advice he would give Senator Bob Dole on debating Bill Clinton

On the Air Force, Unworried

[The Air Force is pleased with the performance of the C-5A cargo plane, although] having the wings fall off at eight thousand hours is a problem.

Major General Charles F. Kuyk Jr.

On the Alamo, Enemy Soldiers We Never Knew Were There

[Alamo defender William Barret Travis] is the guy that with three thousand Russians threatening to attack . . .

Senator Strom Thurmond when campaigning for reelection in his hometown of Edgefield, South Carolina, reminding the audience of local heroes including Alamo defender William Barret Travis

On Alaska, Why the Air Is Really Cleaner

[The following is hereby decreed illegal: all] public flatulence, crepitation, gaseous emission, and miasmic effluence.

bill introduced in Alaska legislature; those farting, or in legalese, flatulating *in public would receive $100 fines*

On Lamar Alexander, Great Ruminations From

Office of the President
University of Tennessee

I would like for us to use "UTK" less. These initials sound as if we were trying to describe the corner of a card catalog in some basement instead of a university trying to be among the best respected in America.

"The University of Tennessee, Knoxville" or "UT, Knoxville" is best. "Knoxville" will work sometimes. Just "UT" works many times. (The sports press—which accounts for 90 percent of the UT, Knoxville media coverage—will always use "UT.") I suppose for some of our documents "UTK" is sometimes inescapable. I try to avoid using "UTK" and I find that I usually can without slighting other campuses.

As for our other campuses, both UT, Memphis and UT, Martin are comfortable with those names. Many people around UT, Chattanooga also use UTC, which in this case is just fine, just as "UVA" and "UCLA" are fine with those circumstances. . . .

This is more important than you might think. . . .

memo written by Lamar Alexander, perennial Republican presidential candidate and then president of UTK or, rather, UT, Knoxville, a.k.a. the University of Tennessee

On Ambassadors, Circular Reasoning Of

... the need to establish a democratic, legal, circular state ...

from a press release put out by the Azerbaijan embassy in London (which was amended the next day with this explanation: "The word 'circular' should be read as 'secular.'")

On Ambassadors, Convincing Qualifications for Becoming

This is the man who was not only the president of the National Council of Shopping Centers, but the *International* Council of Shopping Centers in 1986, and traveled around the world.

Senator Rudy Boschwitz in his recommendation for the appointment of Melvin F. Sembler to the post of ambassador to Australia, as quoted in Spy, *May 1990. Sembler was appointed and confirmed shortly thereafter.*

On Ambassadors In the Know

You mean there are two Koreas?

U.S. ambassador designate to Singapore Richard Kneip, after being asked his opinion during congressional hearings on the North Korea–South Korea conflict

On Americans, Ersatz

Rural Americans are real Americans. There's no doubt about that. You can't always be sure with other Americans. Not all of them are real.

Dan Quayle in a campaign speech

On Answers, a Bit Circuitous . . . Not to Mention Fluid

I see the world in very fluid, contradictory, emerging, interconnected terms, and with that kind of circuitry I just don't feel the need to say what is going to happen or will not happen.

Jerry Brown, former governor of California

On Answers about the Public Eye, Not Too Illuminating

You read what Disraeli had to say. I don't remember what he said. He said something. He's no longer with us.

Former senator Bob Dole (and husband of Republican presidential hopeful Elizabeth Dole) when asked about the Clinton sex scandal and trying to explain how he keeps his private life and public life separate

On Answers about Skipping Military Service, Clear

Reporter Helen Thomas:

If you had it to do over again, would you put on the nation's uniform?

President Bill Clinton:

If I had to do it over again, I might answer the questions a little better. You know, I've been in public life a long time, and no one had ever questioned my role.

On Answers to That Vital Question: What Is a "Salad," As Helpfully Supplied by the Canadian Tax Authorities

Food containing ingredients, whether mixed or not, such as chopped, shredded, diced, sliced, or pureed vegetables, meat, fish, eggs, or other food when supplied with a dressing and/or seasoning(s), whether or not the dressing is mixed with the other ingredients, is considered to be a "salad" for purposes of determining its GST/HST status. A combination of one ingredient and a dressing or seasoning(s), which is sold or represented as a salad, is also considered to be a salad.

All supplies of salads, except those that are canned or vacuum-sealed, are taxable at 7 percent (15 percent in the participating provinces). Generally, if there is no dressing or seasoning applied to the ingredients, and no dressing or seasoning is packaged separately with the ingredients, the package is not considered to be a salad and is zero-rated. However, supplies of fruit salads or gelatin salads are taxable at 7 percent (15 percent in the participating provinces), even though they generally do not contain a dressing. Supplies of salads that are sold in cans or containers that are vacuum-sealed are zero-rated. Supplies of mixed, cut vegetables that are packaged and promoted as "stir-fry" or "chop suey mixes" are also zero-rated, since they are not considered to be salads.

from Canada's General Sales Tax News

On Answers Unanswerable

I challenge my opponent to give a frank affirmative answer: yes or no!
New York mayoral candidate Abe Beame (note: he lost this particular election)

On Anticlimaxes

They have vilified me, they have crucified me. Yes, they have even criticized me.
Chicago mayor Richard J. Daley

On Bad Things to Call Potential Voters

Bums.

President Fernando Henrique Cardoso of Brazil, who was then running for reelection, succinctly stating his thoughts on people who retire early—which didn't go over all that well with the millions of Brazilian pensioners who had begun their working lives when they were children

On Balloons at a Campaign Party, Overwrought Objections To

We don't want balloons—the plastics—the horror!
Doug Heller, media coordinator for the Green Party

On Balls, Vice-Presidential

Bob Hope (holding a golf ball handed to him by President Nixon):
That's great. Thank you. I want that autographed.
President Richard Nixon:
It has the autograph . . . Incidentally, the vice president has one of his balls for you, too.

On Banality, Banal

We talked about mostly where we're going. . . .Towards the future— he and I are both into that, you know.
Representative Newt Gingrich about a conversation he had with President Bill Clinton

On Being a Chauvinist, Obviously

I am not a chauvinist, obviously. . . . I believe in women's rights for every woman but my own.

Chicago mayor Harold Washington

On Benefits, Going Down the . . .

[Spending on federal benefit programs is growing] at an excremental rate.

Representative Frank Guarini (D, N.J.)

The Stupidest Political Name-Calling

Often a politician tries to eviscerate a political foe with a well-turned, pithy phrase. In truth, there is often a touch of the sublime in the ensuing invective—as in Winston Churchill's masterful put-downs.

But what of those politicians who lack that Churchillian touch? Must they suffer in silence? (This is, of course, a rhetorical question.)

In fact, many politicians don't worry about their lack of oratorical skill and instead attack their opponents with gusto rather than finesse. Rather than using rapier-like wit, they employ verbal sledgehammers to turn the trick.

We may consider this, then, a form of political pugilism—and, on reading these finely tuned character assassinations, we may find ourselves happily transported back to our youth . . . and to the playground style of verbal warfare.

On Political Name-Calling

Every lesbian spear-chucker wanted me defeated.
Representative Robert Dornan, after his unsuccessful 1992 campaign for president

On Political Name-Calling, Great Moments In

Power-mongering men with short penises.
speaker of the California State Assembly Doris Allen, succinctly summing up her take on her critics just before retiring from her position

On Not-Too-Smart Names for Political Opponents

Putzhead.
Senator Al D'Amato's succinct off-the-cuff summation of his Democratic opponent Representative Chuck Schumer—who wound up winning the race

On Political Name-Calling, Great Moments In

Congressman Waddler.
Senator Al D'Amato's succinct off-the-cuff summation of the overweight Representative Jerry Nadler (D, N.Y.) (to underscore his point, D'Amato waddled in a circle in front of his audience)

On Biblical Analogies, A Little Far-Fetched

[With Bill Clinton] we have this awesome case of Samson with all of this strength, and yet the special prosecutor, I suppose, would have locked him up.

the Reverend Jesse Jackson, political activist and perennial candidate, on CNN show Both Sides. *After this comment, the Reverend J. Philip Wogaman, pastor of the Methodist church the Clintons attend, threw in his metaphor: "King David did something that was much worse than anything President Clinton is alleged to have done, and King David, if I read my Bible correctly, was not impeached."*

On Big Brother

[The CIA] encourages spouses of intelligence or military agency employees to cooperate with federal investigators in cases where they know or suspect their government-employed husbands or wives are engaged in espionage. Under this provision, the spouse who cooperates in the prosecution or conviction of his or her spouse beloved would be eligible for spousal benefits for life.

CIA proposal as reported in the news media

On Bills, Superpowerful

Mr. Kennard, I believe that this bill does more than just change the law.
Louisiana Representative Arthur Morrel (D, New Orleans) during debate in the Louisiana state legislature

On Bizarre Moments, Senatorial

When you pull the files out, the briefcase closes essentially shut. You can't see in it. I can't see in it. Nobody could see in it.

Senator John Kerry (D, Mass.) defending Clinton after a Republican held up a briefcase and asked how investigators could have missed aide Vince Foster's suicide note

On Blunders, Blind

We're a product of our own blinders.

Patricia Mulroy, general manager, Las Vegas Valley Water District and Southern Nevada Water Authority

On Bombing Ethics

It is unlawful to make civilians or civilian objects the objects of attacks as such. This rule would not be violated by the use of nuclear weapons to attack targets that constitute legitimate military targets.

letter from Clinton administration to the International Court of Justice, explaining the legality of nuclear weapons

On Book Reviews, Cogent

It's a very good historical book about history.

Vice President Dan Quayle on Paul Johnson's Modern Times

On Born in the USA

There appears to be some misunderstanding as to what was meant by the "Native American" category. We were trying to identify persons who are American Indian, Eskimo, or Aleut. . . . Given the relatively large number of members who checked the Native American category, we believe some may have misunderstood the request.

memo from the Washington, D.C., bar, referring to the race/ethnic question on their annual registration form, on which many American-born lawyers identified themselves as Native Americans, not realizing that this referred only to those with immigrant ancestors who made the crossing via Alaska in a previous millennium

On Bottomless Pits, Limited

U.N. goodwill may be a bottomless pit, but it's by no means limitless.
John Major, British prime minister

On Boyish Crushes, Bizarre

With these few words I want to assure you that I love you and if you had been a woman I would have considered marrying you, although your head is full of gray hairs, but as you are a man that possibility doesn't arise.

Ugandan president Idi Amin in a letter to Tanzanian president Nyerere

On Bribes from Foreign Agents, Accepting

I don't see anything unusual about it.

Louisiana governor Edwin Edwards, after admitting that his wife accepted $10,000 from a Korean businessman with ties to the South Korean CIA

On British Women, Absolutely, Totally Straight

We're well aware of the male homosexual problem in this country, which is of course minor, but to our certain knowledge there is not one lesbian in England.

Lord Chamberlain of England to Lillian Hellman during a discussion of the play The Children's Hour *(from* Lilly *by Peter Feibleman)*

On the Buck Stops Here . . . Sort Of

I said I was the captain of the ship and I accept responsibility, even though I did not know anything about what happened in terms of the changing of this picture. I knew nothing about it.

Senator John Warner (R, Va.) referring to the advertising agency he fired for putting together a false photo that showed Warner's opponent shaking hands with Governor Douglas Wilder of Virginia, while President Clinton stood nearby

On Bummers

The last thing you want is for somebody to commit suicide before executing them.

Gary Deland, former Utah director of corrections, about a special holding cell set up for a death row prisoner who was awaiting execution by firing squad

On Bureaucratic-Speak, Reasons For

Secretary of State Alexander Haig:

Because of the fluctuational predispositions of your position's productive capacity as juxtaposed to government standards, it would be momentarily injudicious to advocate an increment.

Aide:

I don't get it.

Haig:

That's right!

On Bureaucrats, Satanic

It has been brought to our attention that in at least one election, employees may have refused to vote because of their religious beliefs; that is, as regards Form NLRB-666 (notice to employees) they interpreted "666" as the NLRB's display of the "mark of the devil." . . . Replacement versions have been ordered.

memo from the Office of the General Counsel, Division of Operations Management

On George Bush, Clarity Of

If you want to have a philosophical discussion, I take your point, because I think it is important that if we—if you presented me with a hypothesis, "you've got to do this or you've got to do that," and I would accept it and understand the political risks that'd be involved if I showed any flexibility at all in even discussing it—I would have to say that—that a—that you make a very valid point in your question, because, as I tried to indicate in my remarks, it's job creation, and that is attraction of capital that is really the best antidote to poverty.

President George Bush at the American Business Conference explaining why the tax burden shouldn't be shifted from producers to consumers

On the Bush Administration, Claims to Fame

Our entire administration opposes chaos and lawlessness.
President George Bush

On Calls to Arms, Stirring

On questions of war and peace there is a societal imperative for caution, but it must be understood that ambivalence is not synonymous with statesmanship and that anxietyship is no substitute for leadership.

Representative Jim Leach (R, Iowa) during the congressional debate about sending troops overseas to the Persian Gulf, as quoted in the Congressional Record *(note: Leach didn't serve in Vietnam; he got a student deferment, then a medical deferment)*

On Campaign Moments, Confusing

Dan Quayle (extending his hand during a campaign stop at Hardee's):
    I'm Dan Quayle. Who are you?
Woman:
    I'm your Secret Service agent.

On Campaigning, Not That Great Moments In

Q:
    What should I tell my friend who can't afford a house in Toronto?
Canadian prime minister Pierre Trudeau (then campaigning for reelection):
    Tell him to move.

On Candidates, Unforgettable

    We've got a strong candidate. I'm trying to think of his name.
    Senator Christopher Dodd, Democratic National Committee cochairman, on Elliot Close, who was going to run for the U.S. Senate from South Carolina against longtime Republican senator Strom Thurmond

On Candidates from Washington, Reasons They Are Not from Washington

I am in Washington, not of it. No insider challenges an incumbent president. That makes me, de facto, an outsider.

candidate Pat Buchanan of Washington, on why he is not a Washington insider

On Capitalism, Great Thoughts About

I think that the free-enterprise system is absolutely too important to be left to the voluntary action of the marketplace.

Congressman Richard Kelly (R, Fla.)

On Chatting with Students, Odd Moments In

Representative Don Young (R, Alaska) (speaking before a group of students in Fairbanks, Alaska, and explaining his position against federal funding of the arts):

[The government has funded] photographs of people doing offensive things.

Q:

Could you give us an example?

Young:

Butt-fucking.

(note: when asked why he would use such dubious terminology, he explained he was just "trying to educate the students")

On Child-Molestation–Free United Nations

By virtue of the authority vested in me as the assistant secretary of state for International Organizations . . . I certify that no United Nations agency or United Nations affiliated agency grants any official status, accreditation, or recognition to any organization which promotes, condones, or seeks the legalization of pedophilia. . . .

State Department document

On Childhood, Long

We have been boyhood friends all of our lives.
Chicago mayor Richard J. Daley

On the Chinese Stealing U.S. Nuclear Secrets, Disingenuous Clinton Defenses

You say they *stole?* Is that the word you used? To the best of my knowledge, no one has said anything to me about any espionage which occurred by the Chinese against the labs during my presidency.
President Bill Clinton, responding to questions that the Chinese stole U.S. nuclear technology

On Chivalry

Chivalry is only reasonably dead.
President George Bush offering a chair to a woman

On Cigarette Smoking, Better Than Cheese or Beer

Wisconsin's economy is intertwined very closely with Philip Morris, and our future is, too.
Wisconsin governor Tommy Thompson

On City Employees, Kinky

[The] morality of city employees is at an all-time low.

Jasper Weese, Traverse City, Michigan, councilman during a City Commission meeting, trying to refer to morale problems

On Civics Lessons from the Former Vice President

There are lots more people in the House. I don't know how many exactly—I never counted—but at least a couple hundred.

Vice President Dan Quayle attempting to explain the difference between the House and the Senate

On Civil Rights, Great Freudian Moments In

This country needs a spear-chucker, and I think we've got him up on this podium.

Eugene Dorff, mayor of Kenosha, Wisconsin, introducing presidential candidate Jesse Jackson. Dorff said later he had intended to say "straight shooter," but slipped.

On Civilization, Insightful Views On

Family is something which goes back to the nucleus of civilization. And the very beginnings of civilization, the very beginnings of this country, goes back to the family.

former vice president Dan Quayle

The Most Adroit Backtracking

Political backtracking is the art of explaining away—in a characteristic backward, crablike scuttling movement—what was done or said yesterday in a fit of candor.

Often, we have a flurry of clarifications, explanations, rectifications, simplifications—all designed for one purpose: obfuscation.

On Calling Someone Putzhead, Quick Thinking About #1

I don't know. I don't remember. It certainly was not for any public, ehh . . . .

Senator Al D'Amato (R, N.Y.) snappily going for the "ignorance" defense, when asked if he had actually called his Democratic opponent, Charles Schumer, a putzhead

On Putzhead, Quick Thinking About #2

I have no knowledge of ever doing it. I just don't. I think it's ridiculous. . . . I would never—I have not engaged in that. I wouldn't engage in it. I haven't done it. Why am I going to do it now?

Senator Al D'Amato trying the denial route

On Putzhead, Quick Thinking About #3

The Yiddish word I used to describe you at a private meeting means "fool."

Senator Al D'Amato in a letter to Chuck Schumer, trying desperately to defuse the issue—which backfired when the press got their hands on the letter

On Putzhead, #4

I stand by my remark one hundred percent.

Senator Al D'Amato still trying to make his "putzhead" comment seem trivial

On Putzhead, #5

You are trying to twist that into a religious slur. . . . I urge you to stop this transparent politically motivated act.

Senator Al D'Amato trying to turn the tables on Schumer by blaming him for creating an uproar

On Illegal Fund-Raisers at Buddhist Temples, Al Gore And

Explanation number 1: It wasn't a fund-raiser, it was a "community outreach event."

Explanation number 2: It wasn't a fund-raiser, it was just "finance-related."

Explanation number 3: It wasn't a fund-raiser, it was a "donor-maintenance meeting."

Vice President Al Gore attempting to explain away his attendance at a Buddhist-temple fund-raiser

On Senator Bob Kerrey, Fancy Footwork Of

Clinton's an unusually good liar. Unusually good. Do you realize that?

Senator Bob Kerrey (D, Neb.) in an Esquire *interview*

It was an unfortunate remark that once it's in print it looks a lot worse than it actually is.

Senator Bob Kerrey commenting on his Esquire *interview to news service AP*

It was not an angry comment. It was actually intended as an off-handed compliment.

Senator Bob Kerrey further explaining to news service UPI

On Clarifications, Clarifying

Technically, they were not used for fund-raising, but they became an element of the financial program that we were trying to pursue in connection with the campaign.

Clinton press secretary Mike McCurry when asked if the White House coffee meetings with wealthy donors were used for fund-raising

On Clarifications, the Tobacco Lobby And

Bob Dole, in speech:

My view is, using drugs is wrong. You shouldn't use drugs. You shouldn't smoke cigarettes. Let's just throw them all out at the same time.

Reporter:

Are you suggesting a ban on cigarettes?

Bob Dole:

Oh, no, come on, you know better than that.

Dole press secretary, a little later:

Actually, Mr. Dole was referring to *marijuana* cigarettes.

On Clarifications, Vital

I talked to the White House this morning. I mean, you can't talk to a building, but I talked to some people in the White House this morning.

George Stephanopoulos, White House aide and now ABC commentator

On Clarifications, Vital

Our mistake:

Liberal MP Sheila Copps did not direct cries of "scumbag" at the Government benches in the House of Commons as reported yesterday. As recorded by Hansard, her comments were, "Who is a scumbag?" followed by, "The honorable member just called us a scumbag."

newspaper correction

On Clarity

I am very clear in my mind that the terminology I have always used as mandatory subjects, which are the subjects that form the mandatory core and curriculum, which means a curriculum guideline with a certain common core that will be used across the province.

Tom Wells, education minister in the Ontario provincial parliament, explaining core curriculum

On Clean Water Act Supporters, Facts About

[They are] the same people that would be homos in the military.
Representative Randy Cunningham (R, Calif.) expressing his opinion on supporters of clean water

On Clear Thinking, Governmental

An agency subject to the provisions of the Federal Reports Act may enter into an arrangement with an organization not subject to the Act whereby the organization not subject to the Act collects information on behalf of the agency subject to the Act.

The reverse also occurs.
memo from the Office of Management and Budget (OMB)

On Clever Political Ways to Say You're Cutting Down National Forests

Hazardous fuels reduction.
from a bill proposed by Representative Helen Chenoweth (R, Idaho), which supposedly would cut the risk of wildfires by allowing timber companies to log in national forests

On Clichés, Cloudy

We see nothing but increasingly brighter clouds every month.
President Gerald Ford talking about the economy to a group of Michigan businessmen

On Clichés, Hypothetical

If a frog had wings, he wouldn't hit his tail on the ground. Too hypothetical.
President George Bush during a 1992 campaign trip to New Hampshire, about extending unemployment benefits

On Clichés, New-Fangled

. . . labor interests may be cutting off their nose despite their face.
from a press release by Representative Nick Smith (R, Mich.)

On Clichés, Simian Political

To use a cliché, we orangutaned the front office. We orangutan the hospitals and bring them into a bill. . . . Let's not kid ourselves. We're orangutaned. That's what we are, brought right in.
Charles F. Sylvia, Massachusetts state representative, on the health-care bill

On Bill Clinton, Clear Statements By

I think that's self-evident, but not true.
President Bill Clinton on criticism that he made conservative speeches but governed as a liberal

On the Clinton Administration, Hidden Goals Of

[We have brought about] the defeat of capitalism.
Clinton treasury secretary Robert Rubin on U.S. role in world affairs

On Clinton Defenses, Not So Great

I think when [Bill Clinton] was governor and not paying proper taxes, he was trying to find sources of income to please [Hillary]. He seeks money for the woman's pleasure, to buy her gifts. Women push men to crime.
Russian politician Vladimir Zhirinovsky

On Bill Clinton, Sensitivity Of

The chart you had was very moving.
President Bill Clinton during a 1992 economic summit, referring to a chart showing income differences between college and high school graduates

On Closure

We will not close any base that is not needed.
Secretary of Defense Les Aspin

On Codes, Multicultural

This code of ethics might solve the problem.
New Jersey state senator Anthony Imperiale, during a debate about a proposed code of ethics

On Coining a Phrase, Odd

[It's] a two-edged coin.
Louisiana state representative Donald Ray Kennard (R, Baton Rouge) attempting to explain how one of his anticrime bills could have a double impact

On Come-Ons, Ones Melanie Griffith Probably Never Heard Before

Do you want to see my dinosaur?
Newt Gingrich to actress Melanie Griffith, when he bumped into her in the hallway while she was at the Capitol lobbying for the National Endowment for the Arts—referring to the Tyrannosaurus rex *bone he kept in his office*

On Comforting Thoughts

Out of fifty-nine thousand students who have graduated from a variety of programs, less than three hundred have been cited for human rights violations, and less than fifty have been convicted of anything.

Major Gordon Martel, U.S. Army spokesman for the Army School of the Americas, defending the school from charges that its graduates rape, loot, and murder civilians

On Comforting Words from District Attorneys

In a sense, the system worked, although it took some time.

Brooklyn, New York, deputy DA Dennis Hawkins on the release of an innocent man who served eight years in prison for murder

On Commissions, Exciting

[I propose to create a] Commission on Erections and Mounting.

Richard M. Daley, mayor of Chicago, proposing to honor the late Everett Dirksen with a statue and to create a commission to look into the matter

On Communism, Proud Boasts About

We are not without accomplishment. We have managed to distribute poverty equally.

Nguyen Co Thach, Vietnamese foreign minister

On Communist Icons, New Style

If there is anyone alive who reminds me of Che today . . . I would say it is Diana, the Princess of Wales.

Fidel Castro in his book proposal for History Will Absolve Me: The Autobiography of Fidel Castro

On the Communist Paradise, Part 1

Our hookers don't do it out of obligation, of necessity. Here, prostitution doesn't occur for that reason but because, somehow, they like it.

Cuban leader Fidel Castro

On the Communist Paradise, Part 2

There is no prostitution in China; however, we do have some women who make love for money.

Chinese Foreign Ministry spokesperson

On Comparisons, Tasteless

He ought to know the difference between a bid and a watermelon.

New York City deputy mayor John Dyson commenting on city comptroller Alan Hevesi and a contract that was being discussed with a black-owned investment firm

On Compassion in Politics

The problem with AIDS is, you got it, you die. So why are we spending money on the issue?

Montana lieutenant governor Dennis Rehberg explaining why he was for cutting spending on hospitals

On Compliments, Not That Great

Ladies and gentlemen, it is my honor to introduce you to the governor of this great state, the Honorable John J. McKeithen and his lovely wife, Marjorie. Look how beautiful she is—every wrinkle in her face is glowing.

New Orleans mayor Vic Schiro introducing the governor and his wife to the city council during a meeting

On Congress, Great Moments in

The motion to lay on the table the motion to reconsider the vote by which the motion to lay on the table the motion to proceed to the consideration of the Fair Housing Bill (HR 5200) was rejected was agreed to.

from December 1980 House session

On Congressional Committees, What They Do, U.S. House of Representatives

To: Members of the Committee on Education and the Workforce . . .

Re: Full Committee and Subcommittee Schedule for the Week of May 25–29, 1998

Monday, May 25, 1998:
The Committee is closed in remembrance of Memorial Day.
Tuesday, May 26, 1998
Nothing is scheduled.
Wednesday, May 27, 1998
Nothing is scheduled.
Thursday, May 28, 1998
Nothing is scheduled.
Friday, May 29, 1998
Nothing is scheduled.

On Congressional Hand-Wringing, Overblown

I have come under some of the most vicious and racist and vile attacks ever seen upon an African-American woman since Harriet Tubman . . . [it's] called persecution, just like they crucified Jesus Christ . . .

Representative Barbara-Rose Collins (D, Mich.)

On Congressional Wisdom

Women are best suited for secretarial work, decorating cakes, and counter sales, like selling lingerie.

South Carolina state representative Larry Koon (R, Lexington)

On Congressional Wisdom

Let me tell you that tolerance is one thing, intolerance another. To be a person intolerant of another person's right to have different views is my idea of tolerance, that is, until that person endeavors to make a public issue of his views.

Congressman Albert Johnson of Washington, chairman of the House Committee on Immigration

On Congressional Wisdom

I make my decisions horizontally, not vertically.
Senator Bob Kerrey (D, Neb.)

On Congressional Wisdom

Those who survived the San Francisco earthquake said, "Thank God, I'm still alive." But, of course, those who died, their lives will never be the same again.
Senator Barbara Boxer (D, Calif.)

The Most Twisted Political Syntax

How do you take a simple sentence and make it virtually incomprehensible? This is best answered by many of our modern politicians, who have made twisted syntax an exuberant new art form.

Presumably all this mangled syntax is a result of years of practice in press conferences, campaign stump speeches, and the like, in which one learns how to say little in many words, to answer questions in a seemingly straightforward but dazzlingly evasive manner, and to generally discover the benefit of speech filled with sound and fury, signifying . . . well, not nothing, but certainly nothing that would prevent election or reelection.

Hence, the proliferation of syntactically challenged speech, complete with dangling verbs, isolated nouns, misplaced tenses, and charmingly incomprehensible clauses—the Gordian-knot school of political communication.

On Defenses, Politically Challenged

The theories—the ideas she expressed about equality of results within legislative bodies and with—by outcome, by decisions made by legislative bodies, ideas related to proportional voting as a general remedy, not in particular cases where the circumstances make that a feasible idea.

Vice President Al Gore on ABC's Nightline, *defending President Clinton's withdrawal of Lani Guinier's nomination*

On Say That Again, Please?

I mean a child that doesn't have a parent to read to that child or that doesn't see that when the child is hurting to have a parent and help out or neither parent there enough to pick the kid up and dust him off and send him back into the game at school or whatever, that kid has a disadvantage.

President George Bush

On Consensual Relations, Special Prosecutor's Take On

White House counsel David Kendall:

One of the purposes [for detaining Monica Lewinsky] was to get Ms. Lewinsky to wear a recording device and surreptitiously record Mr. Jordan or the president, was it not?

Special Prosecutor Kenneth Starr:

It was not . . . we explained to her . . . one of the things a cooperating witness can do is assist us in consensual monitoring.

On Conservatives, Kinky

Joey Bishop, talk show host:

Would you like to become a regular on the show?

Senator Barry Goldwater:

No, thank you. I'd much rather watch you in bed with my wife.

On Conservatives, Mutant

[He is getting support] from the extreme right wing, the extrachromosome right wing.

Vice President Al Gore

On Consistency, Clinton Administration And

George Stephanopoulos on FBI Filegate figure Craig Livingston (in 1994, before Filegate):

He does a terrific job. All I know is that anything that has to do with security or logistics—Craig's going to take care of it. . . . And he knows how to cut through the bureaucracy and get things done.

George Stephanopoulos on Livingston (two years later—after Filegate):

I don't know him that well. He's a guy that was around.

On Conversation, Square

I stand flatly on all four corners of that conversation.

John Erlichman

On Conviction, Political

I think [voters] believe Bob Dole is a good man but he cannot beat Bill Clinton and wouldn't change America if he got the job.

Senator Phil Gramm (R, Tex.) on February 8, campaigning for president

I believe that Bob Dole . . . can make the Republican Party again one united party that is committed to beating Bill Clinton and committed to changing America.

Gramm only ten days later, after withdrawing from the presidential race

On Corpses, Irritated

Where will we get the money to bury the indignant dead?
James McSheehy, member of the San Francisco Board of Supervisors, speaking about his concern for burial of the poor

On Corrections, Communist-Style

In the article "Devote Every Effort to Running Successfully Socialist Research Institutes" (*Sci. Sin.* Vol. 19, no. 5), "the arch unrepentant capitalist-roader in the Party Teng Hsiao-ping" should read "Teng Hsiao-ping."
from the Journal of the Chinese Academy of Sciences, *1977*

On Counting, Presidential Problems With

I hope that history will present me with maybe two words. One is peace. The other is human rights.
former president Jimmy Carter in a Philadelphia Daily News *interview*

On Counting, Prime Ministerial Problems With

The single most important two things we can do . . .

Tony Blair, British prime minister, on BBC1

On Counting, Vice Presidential Problems With

One word sums up probably the responsibility of any vice president. And that one word is "to be prepared."

Vice President Dan Quayle

On Cover-Ups

No one in the White House staff, no one in this administration, presently employed, was involved in this very bizarre incident. . . .What really hurts in matters of this sort is not the fact that they occur, because overzealous people in campaigns do things that are wrong. What really hurts is if you try to cover it up.

President Richard Nixon at the beginning of the Watergate affair

On Covert Operations, As Defined by an Ex-Army Intelligence Officer

The word is not *covert*, it's *overt*. Covert means you're out in the open. Overt is what I did. [Which means] I was undercover.

Chic Hecht, Nevada senator, talking about his eighteen years of participation in covert operations as an Army intelligence officer

On Crime

The streets are safe in Philadelphia, it's only the people who make them unsafe.

Frank Rizzo, ex–police chief and mayor of Philadelphia

On Crime, Interesting Definitions Of

It all depends on what you call crime. If it's a political crime, it's not really a crime.

Political aide Divesh Srivastava on the increase in people with criminal records running for office in India. Srivastava's boss faces twenty-five criminal charges, six of which are for murder.

On Crying During a Live TV Interview, Odd Reasons For

If I don't get my cereal in the morning, I get very emotional.

Elizabeth Holtzman, then New York City comptroller, explaining why, after being asked to sum up her career, she left the live interview in tears and couldn't return for twenty minutes

On Crystal Balls, Cloudy and Odd

This is a long ride. And as I look all the way down the road, I see Dole running out of money, I see Dole not an executive leader, I see Dole without fresh ideas. I see us raising money, I see me with fresh ideas, I see me as an executive leader, and I see a Dole-versus-Alexander race that I can win.

Lamar Alexander while campaigning for the Republican nomination for president

On Culture, Presidential

I'm someone who has a deep emotional attachment to *Starsky and Hutch*.

President Bill Clinton at a meeting with television honchos

On Cut-Rate Problems

[It's a] catch-17.

Louisiana state representative Israel Curtis (D, Alexandria) during a debate in the Louisiana state legislature

On Cute Things to Tell a Female Candidate

[You can win Mayor Guiliani's support by] making him an offer he can't refuse.

Senator Al D'Amato's (R, N.Y.) theoretically humorous joke to Democratic gubernatorial candidate Betsy McCaughey Ross

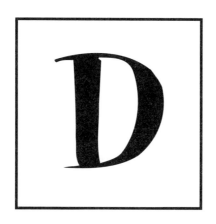

On DA's, Not That Politically Correct

I've never liked young, obese black women, and I think they sense that.

William Tingle, California deputy district attorney, explaining why he was excluding some black women from a jury

On Debating, Use of Vegetables In

I don't want to cast asparagus at my opponent!
unnamed Chicago politician during a debate

On Decisions, Burning

They were torn between two fires.
Congressman John Dent

On Decisiveness, Mario Cuomo And

Mario Cuomo, when asked about the possibility of President Clinton offering him a spot on the Supreme Court:

If an offer were made, I would answer the question so swiftly that every one of you in the media, and especially talk-show hosts, would write, "This, surely, is the most decisive man in America."
Reporter:

Would you accept the offer?
Cuomo:

I don't know what the answer would be.

On Defenses, Not So Great

I hope that Spiro Agnew will be completely exonerated and found guilty of the charges against him.
Texas governor John Connally defending his friend Spiro Agnew

On Defenses, Strong

I have nothing else to say. We—we did—if—the—the—I—I—the stories are just as they have been said. They're outrageous and they're not so.

President Bill Clinton when asked if the stories about his extramarital affairs while he was governor of Arkansas were true

On Definitions, New Governmental

We found the term *killing* too broad.

State Department spokesperson on why the word killing *was replaced with* unlawful or arbitrary deprivation of life *in its human rights reports for 1984–85.*

On Democracies, Different

We have no political prisoners—only Communists [or] people who disagree with our rule.

South Korean president Park Chung Hee

On Democracy, One Representative's View

I can't believe that we are going to let a majority of the people decide what's best for this state.

Representative John Travis, member of the Louisiana legislature from Jackson, when opposing legislation that was popular with voters

On Democracy, Problems With

Democracy used to be a good thing, but now it has gotten into the wrong hands.

Senator Jesse Helms (R, N.C.)

On Democracy, Republican National Convention Definition Of

We are America. Those other people are not.

Republican Party chairman Rich Bond at the 1992 Republican National Convention

On Democracy in Action

You're so damned concerned with what the public thinks that it gets in the way of what's best for us!

Vista, California, city council member Jeanette Smith responding to other council members who were against holding a dinner meeting that would be paid for by the public

On Democracy in Action

Screw the Buddhists and kill the Muslims. And put that in the minutes.
South Carolina State Board of Education member Henry Jordan, explaining how he would deal with groups that objected to displaying the Ten Commandments in public schools. Despite his bold comment, the remarks were deleted from the written minutes, and Jordan later said he didn't mean for his comments to be taken literally.

On Democratic National Convention Speeches, Moving

We're not going to blow it this time. Just shut up, gays, women, and environmentalists. Just shut up. You'll get everything you want after the election. But just, for the meantime, shut up so that we can win.
Congressman Peter Kostmayer (D, Pa.) speaking at the Democratic National Convention.

On Denials, Clear and Convincing

Q:
[Did you have the database installed?]
Hillary Clinton:
I would doubt that I was the person who ordered it.

On Denials, Clear and Convincing

Q:

[Did Clinton lie to you?]

Al Gore:

I've never talked about my private conversations with the president, and I'm not going to start now.

On Denials, Snappy

I deny the allegations and I defy the alligators!

indicted Chicago alderman

On Describing Clothes, Perhaps a Little Too Lasciviously, Part 1

The commander in chief [Clinton] is jogging in San Francisco in his slit-up-the-sides, silk, girlie-girlie jogging pants showing us those beautiful white doughboy thighs of his.

Representative Bob Dornan (R, Calif.)

On Describing Clothes, Perhaps a Little Too Lasciviously, Part 2

I look at Madonna in her see-through red panties and bra, wrapped in the American flag on MTV starting yesterday, telling people how to vote, and I think how can we have a young generation going in such opposite directions . . . .

Representative Bob Dornan (R, Calif.)

On Desert Storm, Hidden Agenda Of

Desert Storm was a stirring victory for the forces of aggression and lawlessness.

Vice President Dan Quayle

The Stupidest Political Metaphors

John Q. Public loves a metaphor . . . or so think politicians. In campaign speeches, press conferences, or off-the-cuff semispontaneous remarks, politicians are prone to the rampant use of metaphors and similes.

In this way, they feel they are simultaneously reaching new oratorical heights, providing snappy sound bites, and connecting with average Americans.

However, something often goes awry twixt metaphor and mouth. And politicians, in their eagerness to slap down a catchy metaphor, wind up, in effect, caught between a rock and the deep blue sea . . . or should that be between the devil and a hard place?

On Animals, Interesting Democratic Observation About
A zebra cannot change its spots.
Vice President Al Gore

On Clichés, a Bit Odd
That's the way the cookie bounces.
New Orleans mayor Vic Schiro, who was famous for his malapropisms—called Schiroisms in New Orleans

On Metaphors, a Little Odd
If we crush the grapes of hope into the raisins of despair, they may not be able to bounce back in the fall.
political activist Reverend Jesse Jackson

On Desexed Language

Senate Agriculture Committee chairman Jesse Helms:

Attaboy, Senator! Atta, uh, girl . . . person . . . what are you anyway?

Senator Paula Hawkins (R, Fla.):

I'm not a person, I'm a lady!

On Desexed Words

[Personhole] is not an acceptable desexed word.

Shirley Dean, councilperson from the Berkeley, California, City Council, explaining why the council had changed the wording in a sewer-equipment request back to "manhole *cover*"

On Deviant Behavior, Weather And

If it [deviant behavior] will bring about terrorist bombs, if it'll bring about earthquakes, tornadoes, and possibly a meteor, it isn't necessarily something we ought to open our arms to.

Pat Robertson

On Difficult-to-Remember Dates

We are trying to change the 1974 constitution, whenever that was passed.

Representative Donald Ray Kennard (R, Baton Rouge) during a debate in the Louisiana legislature

On Diplomacy, Below the Belt

We did a lot of this by the seat of our pants; a lot of this on the fly.

Representative Rod Blagojevich (D, Ill.) commenting on the Jesse Jackson team's successful effort to gain the freedom of the U.S. POWs held in Serbia

On Diplomacy, Great Moments In

Anything concerning the Ambassador's swimming pool must be referred to as water storage tank not as *swimming pool*.

internal State Department memo, U.S. Embassy, Vientiane, Laos

On Diplomacy, Great Moments In

You know, your nose looks just like Danny Thomas's.

President Ronald Reagan to the Lebanese Foreign Minister during a briefing on the realities of the Middle East conflict

On Diplomacy, Great Moments In

I am not wanting to make too long speech tonight as I am knowing your old English saying, "Early to bed and up with the cock."

Hungarian diplomat in a speech to an embassy party

On Diplomacy, Great Moments In

Look, I'm going to tell you something, hon. You've crossed and uncrossed your legs twice, and one time you showed me something I shouldn't see. Now am I going to complain that you're loosey-goosey or you got no class?

U.S. ambassador to Italy nominee Peter Secchia to a female reporter from the Detroit News. *He was later confirmed as ambassador to Italy.*

On Diplomacy, Great Moments In

I'm so proud of my fucking candidate I could shit.

U.S. ambassador to Italy Peter Secchia about George Bush, at a Republican fund-raiser

On Diplomats, Indispensability Of

I'm the consul for information, but I don't have any information.

Ofra Ben Yaacoe, Chicago Israeli consul

On Disabilities, New

Ms. Dobe, an employee of the Labor Department, is appealing a May 22, 1996, written warning issued to her for sleeping at her desk. Ms. Dobe alleged that she had not been given sufficient time since her first warning to correct her problem of sleeping at work. She also alleged that the Department of Labor had an obligation to be more proactive in assisting her with overcoming her "sleeping" problem.

document from the State of New Hampshire Personnel Appeals Board

On Disabilities, Pigmented

Surely, we must be able to find a use for a Swahili-speaking person who has Peace Corps experience, is a cum laude from Harvard, and has a biological background in data manipulation. . . . Unfortunately, Mr. Trevor is white, which is too bad. Would you let me know if you see any prospects?

memo from Office of the Director, Roger Kennedy, of the National Park Service

On Disagreements, Good Reason For

I have to disagree with Mr. Green's amendment because we all probably will go to jail.

Representative B. J. "Buster" Guzzardo (D, Independence) during a debate in the Louisiana legislature

On Distinctions, Dumb

It's not the amendment with which I disagree. It's the contents of the amendment.

Representative Naomi Farve (D, New Orleans) during a debate in the Louisiana legislature

On Distinctions, Important

Being individually hypocritical is a lot different from actually having an important message the nation has to hear.

Colorado governor Richard Lamm advocating H. Ross Perot's participation in presidential debates, even though Perot had refused to debate Lamm during the race for the Reform Party nomination.

On Distinctions We Just Can't See

If you are intent on submitting a final report that makes sense, his testimony becomes essential but not absolutely necessary.

Senator Daniel Inouye, chairman of the Iran-Contra committee, on Oliver North, 1987

On Districts, Chatty

... the only thing that the Federal law on redistricting provides is that the district be congruous and gregarious.

from a government memo

On Disturbing Princely Jokes

Don't stay here too long or you'll go back with slitty eyes.

Prince Philip addressing British students in Beijing, China

On Doing Nothing for Sixty Years

Sixty years of progress, without change.

slogan cooked up by the Saudi Arabian government to celebrate the kingdom's sixtieth anniversary

On Doing Your Part for a Better Government for All

Sexual harassment ... it's everyone's responsibility.

ad published by Administrative and Clerical Officers' Association of Sydney, Australia

On Don't Do As I Do, Do As I Say

The process of contracting out your foreign policy to individuals who don't feel constrained to operate within any policy framework is a very worrisome methodology.

Robert "Bud" McFarlane, former Iran-Contragate political operative—who operated outside of policy frameworks—commenting about Jimmy Carter's nonproliferation deals in 1994

On Downsizing the U.S. Government, Big Plans For

Reporter:

List which federal government departments, if any, you would close.

President Bill Clinton:

The era of big government is over. . . . We plan to eliminate many programs, such as the Tea Tester's Board, Uniformed Service, University of Health Sciences, and the Naval Academy's own dairy farm.

On Drug Abuse, Presidential Take on Stopping

Now, like, I'm president. It would be pretty hard for some drug guy to come into the White House and start offering it up, you know? I bet if they did, I hope I would say, "Hey, get lost. We don't want any of that."

President George Bush talking about drug abuse to a group of students

On Drug Addictions, Presidential Take on Shaking

Did you come here and say, "The heck with it, I don't need this darn thing?" Did you go through the withdrawal thing?

President George Bush questioning a recovering addict while visiting a Newark, New Jersey, drug clinic

On Earth, Where Found

[It's] time for the human race to enter the solar system.
Vice President Dan Quayle on the concept of a manned mission to Mars

On the Economy, Battered

There's not much in either package to really jump-start the economy or blow it out of the water and make it really jump.
Senator Bob Dole (R, Kans.)

On Ecuadorian Presidents, Ones We'd Prefer Not to Know

Madman in Love
title of CD issued by Ecuadorian president Abdala Bucarem

On Education, Indisputable Fact About

More education is not a pancreas.
Mississippi state legislator commenting on a proposed state education plan

On Egos

[My wife] has a very major cause and a very major interest that is a very complex and time-consuming issue with her. And that's me.
Dan Quayle when asked if his wife, Marilyn Quayle, was thinking of becoming involved in a cause

On Egos, Annoying

I have enormous personal ambition. I want to shift the entire planet. And I'm doing it. I am now a famous person.
House Speaker Newt Gingrich

On Election Hints, Helpful

You can get elected by proclaiming that you are a sodomite and engage in anal sex all the time. You will get elected.

Representative Bob Dornan (R, Calif.)

On Election Jokes, We're Not So Sure

Eight more days, and I can start telling the truth again.

Senator Chris Dodd (D, Conn.) on the Don Imus show, on campaigning

On Eloquence, Political

[I condemn] rampart speculation.

Senator Ted Kennedy warning reporters not to jump the gun and speculate about Clinton

On Employment Notices from the Twilight Zone

[Come investigate war crimes in] still beautiful Rwanda, once considered the Switzerland of Africa.

employment notice by U.S. Department of State for war-crimes investigators in Rwanda

On Endangered Airports

Ag land is not sacred. It's a green area on a map. But an airport is a resource that needs to be protected.

Steve Dana, mayor of Snohomish, Washington, during a land-annexation debate

On Endorsements, Not That Great

Except for his tendency to get angry, arrogant, and sulky, he is the most qualified.

Noboru Takeshita, former Japanese prime minister, on trade minister Ryutaro, a candidate for prime minister

On Endorsements by Employees, Ringing

He kept the promises he meant to keep.

George Stephanopoulos on the Larry King show, explaining why he predicted Clinton would win a second term

On Equal Opportunity, Absolutely Fascinating Insights On

When women have equal equipment, they can have equal opportunity.
New Hampshire state representative Warren Henderson (R, Exeter) during a trip on which several people suggested they look for a bathroom so the women state senators wouldn't have to relieve themselves in the woods . . . as some of the men already had

On the Essence of Politics, Great Observations About

Let me turn to California and get parochial. If I do not get parochial, the people will find someone who will.
California state representative Clair Burgener speaking at an energy hearing

On Ethical Excuses by Senators Caught Spending Their Campaign Contributions on Their Car Dealerships

I don't know every damned thing in that ethics law.
South Carolina state senator Robert Ford, accused of the unethical practice of using campaign money for noncampaign purposes— namely, mailing ads for his car dealership in Charleston

The Most Dubious Examples of Political Press Relations

One of the most entertaining aspects of politician-watching is enjoying that form of political torture known as the press conference. Here, politicians submit themselves to questioning to slake the bloodlust of the press—and, ostensibly, to keep the public informed.

And, of course, politicians are only *too* delighted to answer questions, explain problems and dilemmas they are facing, and generally keep the lines of communication open. Well, in *theory,* they are.

On Press Conferences, Great Moments In

Reporter:

Do you know to what extent the U.S. and Colombia are in fact cooperating militarily now, in terms of interdiction efforts?

George Bush:

Well, I—yes, I know that.

Reporter:

Can you share that with us?

Bush:

No.

Reporter:

Why not, sir?

Bush:

Because I don't feel like it.

at a press conference just before Bush was going to attend a drug summit in Colombia

On Great Moments In Press Conferences

Reporter:

Mr. Secretary, has anyone asked you the whereabouts of Mr. Molotov?

Secretary of State Dean Rusk (just back from a Moscow summit):

No. No one has asked me that question. You can if you want to.

Reporter:

Well, sir, where is Mr. Molotov?

Rusk:

I haven't the faintest idea.

On Once Burned

Reporter:

What will be your role in welfare reform?

Hillary Clinton (approaching Christmas decorations):

Smell that gingerbread. You can actually smell it when you get close to it.

On Etiquette, Military Juntas And

It was a mistake. It shows a lack of politeness to kill people when the pope asks us not to do it.

Guatemalan government official on the execution of political prisoners just before the pope's visit

On Exciting Verbal Exchanges in the House

You fucking anti-Catholic! . . . Coward! . . . [Do you want to] step outside?

former representative Bob Dornan (R, Calif.) colorfully rebutting Representative Bob Menendez (D, N.J.), who questioned whether Dornan, who had recently lost his reelection bid, had a right to speak on the House floor

On Excuses, Convenient

I had thought very carefully about committing hara-kiri [ritual suicide] over this, but I overslept this morning.

Former Japanese labor minister Toshio Yamaguchi after being arrested on charges of breach of trust in connection with two failed financial institutions—explaining how upset he was over being only the second member of the Japanese parliament arrested in more than two decades

On Excuses, Pitiful

The Secretary thanks you for bringing this to his attention.

Letter from the staff of U.S. commerce secretary William Daley after he was asked why he didn't pay U.S. Customs duties on his three handmade suits and eight handmade shirts that he bought in Hong Kong

On Excuses for Choking Someone, Extremely Convincing, Part 1

His boss may have needed choking. It may have been justified . . . someone should have asked the question, "What prompted that?"

San Francisco mayor Willie Brown explaining that basketball star Latrell Sprewell shouldn't have been summarily fired for choking and threatening to kill his coach

On Excuses for Choking Someone, Extremely Convincing, Part 2

This is not a person accused of rape, accused of kicking a TV cameraman, accused of carrying a gun on an airplane.

San Francisco mayor Willie Brown explaining why Warriors star Latrell Sprewell, who choked and threatened to kill his coach, wasn't really guilty of anything major

On Excuses That Tax Our Intelligence

[Paying taxes] was one of the things I was always going to take care of, but sometimes I did not have all the funds available or I did not have all the documents and other materials I needed.

David Dinkins, New York City mayor, trying to answer accusations that he failed to pay his taxes

On Explanations, One We're Not Sure We Believe, Thank You

It [the stain on the blue dress] could have been spinach dip or something.

Monica Lewinsky in her grand jury testimony, commenting on the semen stain on her famous blue Gap dress

On Explanations, Ones That Need Explaining

In such jurisdictions, the low HOME rent will have increased and, in some cases, will exceed the high HOME rent. In cases where the low HOME rent exceeds the high HOME rent, the rent applicable to a unit subject to the low HOME rent may not exceed the lower of the rents under §92.252(a)(1), i.e., the applicable high HOME rent.

from a memo by Gordon McKay, Director of the Office of Affordable Housing, U.S. Department of Housing and Urban Development

On Eyesight, Super

If I had ninety-ninety hindsight . . .
President George Bush

On "Facts" about African-Americans They Probably Didn't Know

[African-Americans] aren't leaders. A black man would rather work for a white person.

Joffree Legget, mayor of Trenton, North Carolina

On Facts, Indisputable

Democrats did very well in Democratic primaries.

Dee Dee Myers, then Clinton's press secretary

On Facts, Indisputable

No matter where you go, there you are.

attributed to Toronto municipal politician Allan Lambert during a city council meeting

On Facts, Indisputable

The power of the head of state is not unlimited. Why is it said the power of the president is not unlimited? Probably the idea comes from the English translation: "Is not unlimited."

Speaker of the Indonesian Parliament Kharis Suhud in a TV interview

On Facts, Unfactual

The only thing worse than making you wait for the facts is giving you facts that turn out not to be facts.

Pentagon spokesman Captain Steve Pietropaoli on NATO bombings in Serbia

On the Family That Writes Speeches Together

I am running for governor not because I am George and Barbara Bush's son. I am running because I am George P. and Noelle and Jeb's father.

Jeb Bush announcing his candidacy for governor of Florida

I am not running for governor because I am George Bush's son. I am running because I am Jenna and Barbara's father.

George W. Bush announcing his candidacy for governor of Texas

On the Family That Writes Speeches Together As Well

We need leaders who will summon from each of us the best of our character.

Bob Dole in a 1995 campaign speech

Our people are looking for leaders who will call America to her better nature.

Elizabeth Dole in a 1999 campaign speech

On Family Trips to Paris, Senatorial Insights On

This was not a junket in any sense of the word.

Senator Strom Thurmond (D, S.C.), who took his wife, two children, next-door neighbor, and eight staff members on a five-day trip to the Paris Air Show. Taxpayers footed the airfare.

On Family Values

I think incest can be handled as a family matter within the family.
Representative Jay Dickey (R, Ark.) defending his position against abortion even in the case of rape or incest

On Famous First Words, Ironic

This law . . . is a foundation stone for the trust between the government and our citizens. . . . Opponents called it a tool of partisan attack against Republican presidents and a waste of taxpayer funds. It was neither. In fact, the independent counsel statute has been in the past and is today a force for government integrity and public confidence.
President Bill Clinton on June 30, 1994, upon signing the Independent Counsel Act

On Famous Last Words, Part 1

The other thing we have to do is to take seriously the role in this problem of . . . older men who prey on underage women. . . . There are consequences to decisions.
President Bill Clinton in a June 13, 1996, speech, long before the Monica Lewinsky affair, endorsing a national campaign against teen pregnancy

On Famous Last Words, Part 2

[There is] no question that an admission of making false statements to government officials . . . is an impeachable offense.

President Bill Clinton as quoted in the Arkansas Gazette

On Famous Last Words

I'm glad I'm not Brezhnev. Being the Russian leader in the Kremlin, you never know if someone's tape-recording what you say.

President Richard Nixon

On Fascinating Imagery

Give Bill a second term, and Al Gore and I will be turned loose to do what we really want to do.

Hillary Clinton speaking at a Democratic fund-raiser

On Fascinating Political Bus Observations

It has comfy seats. . . . It has overhead lights. . . . It has a place to store your bag above your head. . . . It has a pouch where you can store things

in front of your feet. . . . It has armrests. . . . It has tinted windows. . . . This, this is so much better than a school bus. . . . How much does it cost?
>*attributed to political activist and actor Alec Baldwin (and possible congressional candidate, according to his aides) during a charter bus trip to Massachusetts where he was going to campaign for campaign-finance reform (as quoted by Stephen Glass in* The New Republic)

On Fast-Food Joints, Beverage Choices In

Counterperson at McDonald's:
>What do you want to drink?

James Buckley, aristocratic candidate for senator:
>What's your house Chablis?

On Faux Pas, Freudian

>Anyone in his position needs to be whiter than white.
>*British MP Dame Jill Knight on South African leader Nelson Mandela*

On Febrile Prognosticating

I have the thermometer in my mouth and I am listening to it all the time.

Northern Ireland Secretary William Whitelaw explaining how he kept tabs on his party's morale during his campaign

On Feminists, Back in the Kitchen

NOW has always encouraged the nourishment of women's minds and souls, so it seems natural for us to write a book about nourishing the body as well.

Political activist and NOW president Patricia Ireland in a press release announcing the publication of a NOW cookbook, Don't Assume I Don't Cook

On Feminists, out of the Kitchen

Dieting for me is an act of feminism.

Susan Estrich, former campaign manager for Mike Dukakis during his presidential run, defending a diet book she recently wrote

On Figuring Out Leap Years, Helpful Government Hints

A Leap Year is determined if the 4-digit year can be divided by 4 UNLESS

The year can be divided by 100, then it is not a Leap Year, UNLESS

The year can be divided by 400, then it is a Leap Year, UNLESS

The year can be divided by 4,000, then it is not a Leap Year, UNLESS

The year is 200 or 600 years after a year that is divisible by 900, then it is a Leap Year.

memo put out by the Ohio Department of Administrative Services

On Firemen, When You Can Bring to School

[Senate Bill 21] broadens the definition of carrying a fireman on school property.

Louisiana state legislature House computer explanation of a particular bill intended to clarify when firearms could be carried on school property

On Firm Stands

[I am] pro-choice with limitations, pro-life with exceptions.
John Warner, senator from Virginia, in a statement kicking off his bid for reelection

On First Ladies as Secret Weapons

We have to find the key to the skills of propaganda learned by Hillary.

Chinese Academy of Sciences, the Journal of Ideological and Political Work Studies

On Flaming Snowballs

If this thing starts to snowball, it will catch fire right across the country.

Robert Thompson, former Canadian Social Credit leader

On Food for Thought

My appetite is so good that I can eat the tablecloth right off the chair.

Representative J. Joseph Moakley (D, Mass.)

On Football Analogies, Bizarre

At the end of the field is a field goal and what if the referee went to move the field goal every inning and carry the ball over the finish line.

Patricia Mulroy, general manager, Las Vegas Valley Water District and Southern Nevada Water Authority, addressing the 41st Annual Colorado Water Congress—and trying to liken the negotiation process with California to a never-ending Super Bowl game

The Best Examples of How Not to Win Votes

There are those politicians who know that they must win friends and influence people—but who, lamentably, lack the necessary finesse. These well-meaning pols, so anxious to please, so eager to identify with their audience, and so keen on winning votes, try earnestly to reach out . . . but somehow, something goes a bit wrong. What they mean to say just doesn't quite come out the right way. And as a result, these politicians wind up emulating not Dale Carnegie, but Don Rickles working a nightclub crowd.

On What Not to Say to an African-American Audience

My heart is as black as yours.

Mario Procaccino, Democratic candidate for New York mayor in 1969, to a black audience

On What Not to Say to a Senior-Citizen Audience

Fortunately, in years past, they died at an earlier age.

Robert A. Cedarburg campaigning for Congress in a speech to senior citizens in St. Louis (After he said this, he added, "Maybe that wasn't well put.")

On Gerald Ford, Little-Known Facts About

Gerald Ford was a Communist.

President Ronald Reagan in a speech. He later indicated he meant to say "congressman."

On Foreign Affairs, Senatorial Grasp Of

What is this Gaza stuff? I never understood that.

Senator William Scott (R, Va.) in a conversation with Israeli prime minister Yitzhak Rabin

On Foreign Affairs Advisers, Twangy

When I need a little advice about Saddam Hussein, I turn to country music.

President George Bush

On Foreign Affairs Knowledge, Prepubescent Prepresidents And

I grew up in a little town in Arkansas that had a substantial Lithuanian population so I grew up knowing a lot about the problems of Baltic nations.

President Bill Clinton

On Foreign Leaders, Great Observations About

And I was with him, and I sensed . . . Stop! And he stopped. And he got out of the car. So he controls the agenda. And I saw that, yeah.

President George Bush, answering a reporter's question about Gorbachev's control of Soviet government

On Barney Frank, Freudian Names For

Barney Fag.

Representative Dick Armey (R, Tex.) to radio reporters, referring to openly gay congressman Barney Frank. (Armey corrected himself and apologized to Frank, but blamed the media for airing an "inadvertent mispronunciation," saying he did "not need any psychoanalysis about my subliminals or about my Freudian predilections, especially from people who are obviously not trained in psychological analysis.")

On Barney Frank, More Names For

Barney Fife.

Democratic political consultant James Carville who, in haranguing Representative Dick Armey for calling Frank "Fag" wound up referring to Frank as Fife—the bumbling Mayberry deputy played by Don Knotts

On Freedom, Often Overlooked Meaning Of

A mere forty years ago, beach volleyball was just beginning. No bureaucrat would have invented it, and that's what freedom is all about.

Newt Gingrich at the 1996 GOP convention

On Freedom of Thought, Great Examples Of

To reject Bill [Lann Lee for the Justice Department] is a hate crime.

activist and candidate Jesse Jackson on Clinton appointee Bill Lann Lee

On Freudian Slips

We need laws that protect everyone. Men and women, straights and gays, regardless of sexual perversion . . . ah, persuasion.

Bella Abzug, New York politician, addressing a rally for the Equal Rights Amendment

On Freudian Slips

But whatever we do with the law, we know that ultimately this is an affair of the heart.

President Bill Clinton at a National Prayer Breakfast, on making it harder to get a divorce

On Freudian Slips

I am sure that this commission will do an infinitesimal amount of good.

Frank G. Bonelli, Los Angeles County Board of Supervisors, welcoming a presidential commission on drug traffic

On Freudian Slips

If we [legislators] don't watch our respective tails, the people are going to be running the government.

Bill Craven, California state senator, discussing the increase in citizens' initiatives—the use of petitions to get proposed laws on the ballot

On Freudian Slips

[I wish you could be here with me in Illinois to see] all these beautiful white people.

Nancy Reagan talking to her husband, Ronald Reagan, via a phone call that was being broadcast to the crowd, during a campaign trip to Illinois . . . which had just been hit by a sixteen-inch snowfall

On Freudian Slips

She's a wonderful, wonderful person, and we're looking forward to a happy and wonderful night—uh, life.

Ted Kennedy, Massachusetts senator, to the South Shore Chamber of Commerce about his fiancée, Victoria Reggie

On Freudian Slips

My colleagues and I are upset by this blatant attempt to replace diversity with fairness.

Joseph Doria, Democratic leader in the New Jersey State Assembly, on a bill repealing racial and gender preferences; as quoted in the New Jersey Law Journal *(Not surprisingly, he later denied saying this.)*

On Freudian Slips

[We should] vote against Congressman Kennedy's annulment . . . I mean amendment.

Representative Mike Pappas (R, N.J.) about legislation proposed by Representative Joseph P. Kennedy, who had just asked the Catholic Church to grant him an annulment after many years of marriage . . . and children

On Freudian Slips

I think it's eminently fair we be allowed to present at least one witness . . . and that is Monica LeWitness.

Representative Bill McCollum (R, Fla.) arguing that witnesses should be called during the Clinton impeachment hearing and falling prey to a slip of the tongue—one that he quickly corrected

On Freudian Slips

I think he [Bill Clinton] should have made it very clear to Monica, to her family, all those forces need to feel that there's no fall guy. The responsibility should have been in his lap.

the Reverend Jesse Jackson, perennial candidate and political activist, on the Monica Lewinsky scandal

On Freudian Slips

He [President Clinton] should lay it on the table and let the American people decide.

congressman overheard commenting on Clinton sex scandal

On Freudian Slips, Fishy-Horsy

I've bought horses before. I've bought horse races before. I mean . . .
Louisiana state senator Ken Hollis (R, Metairie) discussing a horse-racing bill

On the Future, Fascinating Insights About

Things happen more frequently in the future than they do in the past.
Washington governor Booth Gardner

On the Future, Where It Is

It's a question of whether we're going to go forward into the future, or past to the back.
Vice President Dan Quayle

On Gangsta Rappers, Liddy Dole And

Elizabeth and I are especially excited about the news of your nomination because we will have the chance to be with you.

Bob and Elizabeth Dole in a letter to rap star Eazy-E of gangsta rap group NWA (Niggers with Attitude), informing him of his nomination to the Republican Senatorial Inner Circle

On Gay Rights, Etc., Why They're Bad for Agriculture

American Christian values have encouraged farming. I see the cultural upheaval we're in right now as an attack against farming.

Jim Gordon, real estate developer running for the Republican nomination for South Carolina state commissioner of agriculture

On Geese, Bureaucratic

Don't go around killing the goose that provides the golden opportunity.

attributed to Toronto municipal politician Allan Lambert during a city council meeting

On Gender Differences, Key Points About

If combat means living in a ditch, females have biological problems staying in a ditch for thirty days because they get infections. . . . On the other hand, men are basically little piglets: you drop them in a ditch, they roll around in it—it doesn't matter, you know. These things are very real.

Newt Gingrich, in a lecture on "Renewing American Civilization"

On Gender Identification Problems, Bill Clinton And

President Bill Clinton (paying tribute to heroic pilot Gail Halvorsen, in a speech commemorating the fiftieth anniversary of the Berlin Airlift):

[And] she is with us today.

(The seventy-seven-year-old Gail Halvorsen, a grandfather and clearly a male, stands.)

Clinton (embarrassed):

Thank you, *sir.*

On Gender Identification Problems, George Bush And

Yes, ma'am? Right here, this lady. No—she! Yes—right—second row [pointing]. Next to the guy in the blue shirt, holding her left hand up. It's a he—sorry about that. Gotta be careful. I'm very sorry. Go ahead! I'm— excuse me—I'm very sorry. Go—ah—I—a thousand apologies—go ahead.

President George Bush at a press conference, mistaking genders

On Geopolitical Knowledge, One Candidate's Odd Grasp Of, Part 1

. . . NATO and its allies and the United States.

Texas governor George W. Bush forgetting that the United States is in NATO

On Geopolitical Knowledge, One Candidate's Odd Grasp Of, Part 2

Grecians . . . Kosovanians.

Texas governor George W. Bush attempting to refer to Greeks and Kosovars

On Getting Rich, Why You Shouldn't Bother

There's no way to make everybody rich. I don't even know if it's worth the trouble because the life of a rich person, in general, is very boring.

Fernando Henrique Cardoso, Brazilian president, who was then running for reelection, in a speech in the Parque Royale slum outside of Rio. He followed this up by saying he was a working man and didn't consider himself wealthy (even though his income was in the top 2 percent for Brazilians).

On Getting the Vote Out, New Insights On

A low voter turnout is an indication of fewer people going to the polls.

Vice President Dan Quayle

On Girls, Helpful Senatorial Tips For

Girls shouldn't play with men's balls. Their hands are too small.

Senator Wally Horn of Iowa talking about girls sports in school—and specifically, what size basketball they should play with

On Global Thinking, Redundant

The world has gone through tremendous change recently; both nationally and internationally.

British prime minister John Major

On Good Old-Fashioned Volunteering, How Much Money You Make

Volunteer [and] get labor and family-friendly candidates elected this November.

You will be reimbursed for each four hours volunteered.

AFL-CIO in Iowa

On Al Gore, Precocious Computer Genius Of

Newsman Wolf Blitzer:

Why should Democrats, looking at the Democratic nomination process, support you instead of Bill Bradley, a friend of yours, a former colleague in the Senate? What do you have to bring to this that he doesn't necessarily bring to this process?

Vice President Al Gore:

During my service in the United States Congress, I took the initiative in creating the Internet.

from a CNN interview

On the Government, Congressional Knowledge of

There are four departments. There's the executive, and the legislative, and the judicial, and—the Bill of Rights.

Senator Kenneth S. Wherry of Nebraska

On Government, Presidential Knowledge of the (Supposed) Branches Of

You know we have three great branches of this government of ours. . . . We have a strong president, supposedly in the White House. We have a strong Congress, supposedly in the legislative branch. We have a strong Supreme Court, supposedly heading the judiciary system.

President Gerald Ford

The Most Unusual Political Stances

Some politicians march to the beat of a different drummer . . . a *very* different drummer. Rather than come up with the same old tired legislative proposals, they opt for innovation—and, much like Captain Kirk, boldly go where no man has gone before. These pioneering pols are responsible for the following examples of truly . . . *unusual* legislation. One certainly cannot argue with their individualism; as for their efficacy . . . well, this may be another matter.

On Crime-Fighting Ideas, Not So Great

One of my constituents suggested we amputate trigger fingers. The people are way out in front of the politicians on the crime issue.

Washington state representative Ida Ballasiotes

On Drug Laws, Enlightened

[Pot smokers will be punished by the amputation of the arm or leg. Convicted person and court must agree on] which body part shall be removed.

from a bill proposed by Mississippi state representative Bobby Moak

On Hurricanes, Fascinating, Little-Recognized Benefits Of

In coastal regions like here, hurricanes have always been a great source of water. It's an alternative source that I don't think the city has given much thought to.

Tom Nix, Corpus Christi mayoral candidate, explaining why he was against a city proposition to buy water from an irrigation company— and saying that a "good hurricane" might make it totally unnecessary

On Government Handouts, What People Really Want

People don't want handouts! People want hand jobs!
Connecticut governor William O'Neil at a political rally, followed by riotous applause

On Government Press Releases, Honest

Phase 2 of the scheme is to install 3.5 kilometres of paperwork from Highmoor Cross to Nettlebed Reservoir.

Thames Water (an English public utility service)

On Government Spending, Essential

New items on the Internet Tax Freedom act:

—Mark O. Hatfield Fellows Program (Portland State U)—$3 million

—Paul Simon Public Policy Institute (Southern Illinois U)—$3 million

—Howard Baker School of Government (U of Tennessee)—$10 million

—John Glenn Institute for Public Service and Public Policy (Ohio State)—$6 million

On Government Workers We'd Rather Not Meet

[My budget employees] are the kind of people that run over dogs. [Pause] I meant that in the best possible way.

Reagan administrator James Miller

On Grasping Key Political Points

Sooner or later, I need to begin to do what any candidate does in a presidential race. I need to begin to win.

Lamar Alexander, perennial presidential candidate

On Great Moments in Counting, Presidential

Mr. Nixon was the thirty-seventh president of the United States. He had been preceded by thirty-six others.

President Gerald Ford

On Great Moments in Diplomacy

I was thinking of you last night, Helmut, because I watched the sumo wrestling on television.

President Bill Clinton at a Belgian cocktail party to the very robust Helmut Kohl

On Great Moments in Diplomacy

Boy, they were big on crematoriums, weren't they?
President George Bush on an Auschwitz tour in 1987

On Great Moments in Legislation

A law proposed by Missouri state representative Fred Williams in 1984 would have put a $200 fine for blowing one's nose in a "loud, obnoxious, or offensive manner."

Williams:

"I've had to get out of a restaurant to keep from throwing up."

On Great Moments in Legislation

Louisiana state representative Reggie Dupre (D, Montegut):

I can't accept this amendment, Mr. Speaker Pro Tempore.

Louisiana House Speaker Pro Tempore Peppi Bruneau (R, New Orleans):

The amendment is by you, Mr. Dupre.

conversation during a 1997 Louisiana state legislative session

On Great Moments in Speechmaking

On this hill, in these chambers, on this occasion, with my colleagues, and as a man of the House, I feel as if I should remove the feet and the shoes and lay my garments on an altar, because to me the congress of the United States is a shrine to the greatest democracy in the history of the world.

Jack Kemp at a campaign rally of Republican senators in Washington, speaking as a VP candidate

On Great Moments in Speechmaking

Ladies and gentlemen, it is a great pleasure to be with you today. For immediate release only.

New Mexico senator Joe Montoya at a dinner speech in Albuquerque. He had rushed in late and read straight from his press release.

On Great Moments in Speechmaking

Ladies, I have here some figures which I want you to take home in your heads, which I know are concrete.

James McSheehy, member of the San Francisco Board of Supervisors and chairman of the Finance Committee, speaking to a group of San Francisco women

On Great Moments in Speechmaking

My friends, no matter how rough the road may be, we can and we will never, never surrender to what is right.

Vice President Dan Quayle speaking to the Christian Coalition about the need for abstinence to avoid AIDS

On Great Political Stands

Obviously I don't support it, but I support the impulses that are giving rise to it.

President Bill Clinton on the balanced-budget amendment

On Great Reasons to Put Oil Wells in State Parks

There would be no greater joy than to see a beautiful park that our children and adults can go to and learn about the oil and gas industry.

Tony Sanchez, former Texas Parks and Wildlife commissioner and oilman

On Grizzly Bears, Psycho
They are schizophrenic, manic-depressive animals. I don't want them at all in Idaho.

Representative Helen Chenoweth (R, Idaho) explaining why she opposed a plan to reintroduce grizzly bears to her state

On Groundbreaking Laws, Part 1
One can't tolerate certain sights. From next summer, there will be no more flab all over the place: buttocks, cellulite thighs, and drooping boobs will all be banished.

Andrew Guglieri, mayor of Diano Marina, Italy, announcing his hopes to ban certain women from wearing bikinis in town

On Groundbreaking Laws, Part 2
Women with revolting, large, disfigured, flabby, and oblong breasts . . .
from a proclamation issued by Giovanni Petrillo, mayor of the small Italian beach town of Pantelleria, preventing certain women from sunbathing nude

On Groupies, Gore-ing

I'm a really big fan!

Vice President Al Gore to Courtney Love at a Hollywood party. She later told Spin *magazine, "I was like, 'Yeah, right. Name a song, Al.'"*

On Gun Control, Vital Point About

Women are hard enough to handle now without giving them a gun.

Senator Barry Goldwater talking about women in the armed services

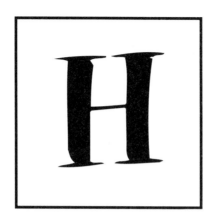

On Hair, Politically Correct References To

Clayton Williams, Republican candidate for governor of Texas:

I sure do like your pigtails.

Native American director of the Inter-Tribal Center:

This is a traditional hairstyle and we call them braids.

Williams:

Well, I think your pigtails are real cute.

On Hairy Palms, Why It's All Clinton's Fault

[Clinton hired] Joycelyn Elders as his surgeon general. The whole point was to have an advocate for weird alternative lifestyles. This administration has had as a policy goal the public discussion of weird sex. He didn't fire Joycelyn Elders until after she said some really weird things and said them many times. She talked about self-abuse. Sex when you're alone.

Representative Chris Cannon (R, Utah) on President Clinton

On Hawaii, Insightful Comments On

Hawaii has always been a very pivotal role in the Pacific. It is in the Pacific. It is a part of the United States that is an island that is right here.

Vice President Dan Quayle

On Hearing, Extraordinary

The honorable member disagrees. I can hear him shaking his head.

Canadian prime minister Pierre Trudeau during a House of Commons session

On Jesse Helms, Great Moments for a Tobacco Senator And

I was with some Vietnamese recently, and some of them were smoking two cigarettes at a time. That's the kind of customers we need!

Senator Jesse Helms on his meeting with the Vietnamese ambassador designate, at a dinner given by the R. J. Reynolds company

On Jesse Helms, Scientific Knowledge Of

Let me tell you something about this AIDS epidemic. There is not one single case of AIDS reported in this country that cannot be traced in origin to sodomy.

Senator Jesse Helms during a debate on an AIDS research and testing bill that guaranteed confidentiality for those testing positive for HIV

On Helpful Government Hints on Why Not to Worry About Radiation

All you have to do [to protect yourself from radiation] is go down to the bottom of your swimming pool and hold your breath.

David Miller, Department of Energy spokesperson

On High Crimes and Misdemeanors, Ones Kenneth Starr Didn't Catch

A number of items were removed from staterooms on the ship [USS *George Washington*] during the White House trip. The following items are unaccounted for: thirteen blue towels with GW [George Washington] insignia—$1 each; four GW bathrobes with insignia—$35 each; twelve plain white bathrobes—$15 each; fifty-five white towels—$.80 each.

from a memo sent by White House staff members to other members, asking that items removed—or stolen—from a navy ship during a White House entourage trip be returned.

On Hints from Nixon, Not Good

If the wife comes through as being too strong and too intelligent, it makes the husband look like a wimp.

former president Richard Nixon advising the Clinton campaign on Hillary

On Historic American Documents, Presidential Knowledge Of

The last time I checked, the Constitution said "of the people, by the people, and for the people." That's what the Declaration of Independence says.

President Bill Clinton criticizing antigovernment rhetoric during his campaign. The quote actually comes from Lincoln's Gettysburg Address.

On Historical Knowledge, Vice-Presidential

Who are these guys?

Al Gore referring to the busts of Jefferson, Washington, Franklin, and the Marquis de Lafayette on a televised tour of Monticello, home of Thomas Jefferson, as CNN cameras rolled

On History, Al Sharpton's Grasp Of

White folks was in caves while we was building empires. . . . We taught philosophy and astrology and mathematics before Socrates and them Greek homos ever got around to it.

the Reverend Al Sharpton in a 1994 speech at Kean College, New Jersey, as transcribed by The Forward

On Homages, Depressing

With the retirement of Dickie Bird, something sad will have gone out of English cricket.

British prime minister John Major

On the Home of All Humankind, Russell, Kansas

I was born, like everybody else here, in a little town of Russell, Kansas.

Senator Bob Dole in a Bakersfield, California, speech

On Honesty in Government, Problems With

My problem was, I was too honest with you the first time.

Representative Tillie Fowler (R, Fla.) to her constituents, explaining why she had changed her mind about term limits

On How Not to Attract New Staffers

There are a bunch of other rats lining up to jump on board.

Vermont congressional candidate Susan Sweetser after a shuffle in her top staff during her campaign

On How Not to Win the Asian Vote

Senator Al D'Amato (R, N.Y.) (in an Asian accent):

Judge Ito loves the limelight. He is making a disgrace of the judicial system. Little Judge Ito. For God's sake, get this thing over. I mean, this is a disgrace. Judge Ito with the wet nose. And then he's going to have a hung jury. Judge Ito will keep us from getting television for the next year.

On How Not to Win the Female Vote

I don't think [women are] temperamentally adjusted to executive positions. They come at problems from a different direction than men do. Women, in my estimation, don't see the practical effect of what they do. . . . Do you want government to be run by your mother?

Phil Marcuse on his female opponent, campaigning for executive of Oakland County, Michigan

The Most Tortured Bureaucratese

A good bureaucratic memo says in fifty words what could easily have been said in ten. But a truly sublime bureaucratic memo aims higher—it seeks to break through normal levels of prolixity and redundancy, and to waste time, effort, and taxpayer dollars on a massive scale.

Consider the following, a memo that could easily be condensed to five or so words—but that would, of course, be unbureaucratic.

On Why Not Just Say "Get Rid of the 'ing'"?

The following Air Force Materiel Command (AFMC) units . . . are redesignated as indicated.

Current Designation	New Designation
377th Civil Engineering Squadron	377th Civil Engineer Squadron
HQ 645th Civil Engineering Group	HQ 645th Civil Engineer Group
645th Civil Engineering Operations Squadron	645th Civil Engineer Operations Squadron
645th Civil Engineering Maintenance Squadron	645th Civil Engineer Maintenance Squadron
647th Civil Engineering Squadron	647th Civil Engineer Squadron
648th Civil Engineering Squadron	648 Civil Engineer Squadron
649th Civil Engineering Squadron	649th Civil Engineer Squadron
650th Civil Engineering Operations Squadron	650th Civil Engineer Operations Squadron

651st Civil Engineering Squadron	651st Civil Engineer Squadron
652nd Civil Engineering Squadron	652nd Civil Engineer Squadron
653rd Civil Engineering Squadron	653rd Civil Engineer Squadron ... etc.

memo from Dennis M. Boggs, Acting Chief, Manpower and Organization, Department of the Air Force

---

On How Not to Win Minneapolis Voters

[These two congressmen are] the education team that Missouri needs to move into the twenty-first century.

Vice President Al Gore at a Minneapolis fund-raiser, trying to honor two Democratic congressmen from Minnesota

On How Representatives Address One Another during House Debates

[You're a] gutless chickenshit.

then House Majority Whip Tom DeLay (R, Tex.) during a campaign-finance-reform debate

On How to Break the News to Your Wife

You're not going to believe this, but ...

President Bill Clinton's first words to Hillary on the Lewinsky scandal according to Hillary Clinton herself in a Today *show interview*

On How to Get a Bill Passed, Non-PC Thoughts On

[I've told State Senator Zaffirini] that if she'll cut her skirt off about six inches and put on some high-heeled shoes, she can pass any [bill] she wants to.

Texas lieutenant governor Bob Bullock, about state senator Judith Zaffirini of Laredo

On How to Get Ahead, Republican-Style

We, as Republicans, need to start rowing with one oar.

Representative John Kasich (R, Ohio) in a Chicago Sun-Times *article on how his party could regain political initiative*

On How to Prove You're on Your Toes about Foreign Affairs

Who?

Ronald Reagan, then Republican candidate for president, when asked about French president Valéry Giscard d'Estaing on a Today *show interview*

On How to Win Voters and Influence People

I like what Kevorkian said. I think in *George* magazine he says, "Maybe nature creating human beings is the pestilence to destroy the world." We're just the f-ing bubonic plague with legs, man.

Geoffrey Feiger, formerly Jack Kevorkian's lawyer, in a comment he made two years before he ran for governor of Michigan . . . but one that kept coming back to haunt him during his campaign

On Huh? Part 1

I think there were some differences, there's no question, and still will be. We're talking about a major, major situation here. . . . I mean, we've got a major rapport—relationship of economics, major in the security, and all of that, we should not lose sight of.

President George Bush on trade talks with Japan

On Huh? Part 2

It gets into quota, go into numerical, set numbers for doctors or for, it could go into all kinds of things.

President George Bush

On Human Life, the Human Part and the Nonhuman Part

[I will try to awaken everyone to] the human dimension of our lives.
Hillary Clinton on her new syndicated column

On Human Resources Theories, Enlightened

Women are lazy and they expect sympathy and they want the jobs just because they're women.

Toronto alderman Joe Piccinnini explaining why there were so few female city employees

On Human Rights, Great Moments In

You hear about constitutional rights, free speech, and the free press. Every time I hear these words I say to myself, "That man is a Red, that man is a Communist!" You never hear a real American talk like that.

Mayor Frank Hague, Jersey City, New Jersey, 1938

On Hunky-Dory, Euphemisms For

I'm confirmed; I'm not looking for a job. It's all loosey-goosey now.
Donna Shalala, Secretary of Health and Human Services

On Hurricanes, Odd Reasons For

I would warn Orlando that you're right in the way of some serious hurricanes, and I don't think I'd be waving those [gay pride] flags in God's face if I were you.

Pat Robertson on his TV show, The 700 Club, *after the Orlando City Council voted to allow gay organizations to hang rainbow flags—a sign of gay pride—from the town's flagpoles to show support for diversity*

On Husbands, Dreamy

If my wife wanted me to use her maiden name, I'd tell her to take it and get out of the house.

Representative J. Louis LeBanc

On Husbands, Great Ones to Have

Like most women, my wife thinks with her glands, not with her head.

Senator Mark Hatfield (R, Oreg.)

On IF U CN RD THS, U CN B A PLTCN 2

I don't have the brains for [business]. I want to go into politics.
Mao Xinyu, grandson of Mao Zedong, laying out his career plans in a Washington Post *interview*

On Imagery, Perhaps a Trifle Embellished

Last time I saw [Bill Clinton] he was swinging on the chandelier in the Oval Office with a brassiere around his head, Viagra in one hand and a Bible in the other, and he was torn between good and evil.
Representative James A. Traficant Jr. (D, Ohio)

On Independent Thinkers
The president doesn't want any yes-men and yes-women around him. When he says no, we all say no.

Elizabeth Dole, then assistant for public liaison to President Reagan, later presidential candidate

On the Ins, Nonpartisan Nature Of
Lower the standards for citizenship. . . . INS management has *already begun* training new adjudicators, and "reeducating" the older ones to be more liberal. . . . [We should] naturalize everyone who filed for citizenship prior to April 1, 1996, in time for them to register to vote in the November election.

memo and letter from the INS (Immigration and Naturalization Service) proposing to make it easier for potentially Democratic aliens to become citizens before the November elections

On Insights, Indisputable
I cannot say and do not know whether the coming quota will be the same, more, or less than the previous one. But the tonnage will definitely fall within one of these three options.

Japanese ambassador to Australia Yoshio Okawara, commenting on the beef quota

On Intermediary, Tricky, Complex Definition Of

Lott is not denying that Morris is calling, and when he is here, he takes the calls. But he is not an intermediary between Lott and Clinton. He calls the president and the president calls him.

Trent Lott spokesman denying that former Clinton adviser Dick Morris was an intermediary between him and Clinton

On International Relations, Great Moments In

Everybody likes to go to Geneva. I used to do it for the Law of the Sea conferences and you'd find these potentates from down in Africa, you know, rather than eating each other, they'd just come up and get a good square meal in Geneva.

Senator Ernest F. Hollings (D, S.C.) on African diplomats who traveled to Geneva to take part in the just concluded international trade agreement talks

On Irreversibility, Reversibility Of

I believe we are on an irreversible trend toward more freedom and democracy. But that could change.

Vice President Dan Quayle

On the IRS, Why Not to Worry About

I want to be sure he is a ruthless son of a bitch, that he will do what he's told, that every income tax return I want to see I see, that he will go after our enemies and not our friends. Now it's as simple as that. If he isn't, he doesn't get the job.

Richard Nixon talking about his criteria for selecting the new IRS commissioner, 1971

On the IRS, Wisdom Of

Passive activity income does not include the following: Income for an activity that is not a passive activity.

IRS Form 8583, Passive Activity Loss Limitation

On It Depends What the Meaning of <u>Nobody</u> Is

Nobody wants to get this matter [about Monica Lewinsky] behind us more than I do, except maybe all the rest of the American people.

President Bill Clinton

On It Depends What the Meaning of the Word <u>Sold</u> Is

Written by President Bill Clinton on a memo from then–Democratic finance chairman Terence McAuliffe outlining a plan to give those who donated the most to the Democratic Party coffees, dinners, golf outings, and more:

Yes, pursue all 3 and promptly—and get other names at 100,000 or more, 50,000 or more. Ready to start overnights [at the White House] right away. Give me the top 10 list back along with the $100[000], $50,000 [donors].

President Bill Clinton, responding to critics who said he had allowed access to special White House trips, etc., in exchange for campaign funds:

The Lincoln Bedroom was never "sold." That was one more false story we have had to endure.

On It's All Women's Fault

Women who refuse to civilize men are responsible for the decline of civilization.

California state senator John Schmitz

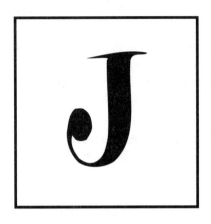

On Jesus, Not Great Vote-Getting Descriptions Of

Jesus is just some goofball who got nailed to the cross.

Geoffrey Feiger, Democratic candidate in the Michigan gubernatorial race (and formerly Jack Kevorkian's lawyer), made this comment two years before running for office . . . but kept hearing about it throughout his campaign

On John Travolta Films, Favorite

. . . that one about dancing, about twenty years ago, *Saturday Night Live.*

Senator Al D'Amato (R, N.Y.)

On Jokes, Cute, Lighthearted

I come back from Africa to stained dresses and cigars and this and impeachment. I am thinking to myself, in other countries they are laughing at us twenty-four hours a day and I'm thinking to myself, if we were in other countries, we would all, right now all of us together, all of us together would go down to Washington and we should stone Henry Hyde to death! Wait! Shut up! Shut up! No, shut up! I'm not finished. We would stone Henry Hyde to death and would go to their homes and we'd kill their wives and children. We would kill their families!

actor and political aspirant Alec Baldwin on the Conan O'Brien show, commenting about the impeachment to the cheers of the audience—and to the shock of many viewers and members of the media. When later asked about the propriety of Baldwin's "joke," his spokesman suggested that critics "lighten up." But Baldwin later apologized to Hyde and explained that his words were supposed to be a parody of "the kind of hate-mongering, crowd-baiting rhetoric that seems to prevail on television these days."

Great Moments in Nonpolitical Correctness

Political correctness has taken much of the spice out of politics. In the estimable interests of not offending anyone, savvy politicians now employ modern desexed pronouns, speak only of hyphenated Americans, and insult political enemies in the most careful—and colorless—language.

But every so often there comes along what we may politely call an old-fashioned politician—others may prefer another term— a politician unafraid of charges of sexism, racism, ageism, or, in fact, any other ism. This politician confidently calls 'em as he (he is, alas, almost inevitably male) sees 'em, and damn the consequences!

On Charm and Couth, Congressional

She has the *beeeg* breasts.
Representative Martin Hoke (R, Ohio) before getting ready to comment on Clinton's State of the Union address, referring to a comely producer walking by (Hoke didn't realize his mike was turned on, among other things)

On Ethnic Sensitivity, Great Moments In, Part 1

Representative Sidney Yates (D, Ill.) speaking to Hispanic high school students:

Do you own sombreros?
Do you know the Mexican hat dance?

On Ethnic Sensitivity, Great Moments In, Part 2

Representative Sidney Yates (D, Ill.):

[I don't see why they were so] offended. I enjoy the Mexican hat dance. I bought one of those big sombreros on vacation a few years ago.

On How Not to Win the Irish Vote

Whoever designed the streets must have been drunk. . . . I think it was those Irish guys.

Minnesota governor Jesse Ventura, commenting on the often-confusing streets in St. Paul (he later apologized for his comment)

On Jokes, Dubious

Bad weather is like rape. If it's inevitable, just relax and enjoy it.

Clayton Williams, then Republican candidate for governor of Texas

On Jokes, Dubious—Bad Attempts at Explaining Them Away

That was a joke. It wasn't a serious statement. . . . If anyone's offended, I apologize. . . . This is not a Republican woman's club that we're having. It's a working cow camp—a tough world where you get kicked in the testicles if you're not careful. It's a different world.

Clayton Williams, trying to defuse the situation after his infamous "rape" joke—and digging himself in deeper and deeper. A day later, he accepted the inevitable (to use his phrase)—"I apologize from the bottom of my heart," he said.

On Jokes, Municipal-Government-Style

For those homeless who are dually diagnosed (mentally disabled and a drug abuser), a special euthanasia program is essential.

from an official draft of the Irvine, California, Comprehensive Housing Affordability Study; embarrassed city officials explained that it was simply someone's idea of a joke

On Jokes, Real Knee-Slappers

Caption on a photo of a mushroom cloud:

Built in the U.S. by lazy, illiterate Americans . . . tested in Japan.

Sent (along with other materials such as fake tax forms for homeless people saying "please identify Dumpster locations") by Texas state representative Will Hartner (Dallas) to his Republican colleagues. When questioned about the mushroom-cloud statement, he replied, "Obviously if you don't like nuclear warfare, you're not going to like that."

On Journalists, What Politicians Really Think

Journalists are not supposed to ask questions.

Singapore liaison for International Trade Minister Datuk Seri Rafiday, at the airport, when confronted with journalists (She quickly added, "Except at press conferences," after seeing the incredulous looks of the journalistic audience.)

On Jumping the Gun, the Doles And

And then he [Clinton] gave you the big medical care plan, the president, I mean Elizabeth, President Dole talked about, Elizabeth Dole talked about—she probably will be the next president. But in any event, that's the way it works.

Senator Bob Dole in a campaign speech in Tennessee

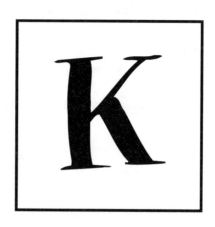

On Kansas City, the Ideal of All Cities

We will lift Shanghai up and up, ever up, until it is just like Kansas City.

Senator Kenneth Wherry (R, Nebr.)

On Ted Kennedy, In-Depth Musical Knowledge Of

The music of you and your brothers has been an inspiration to millions.

Senator Ted Kennedy to talk-show host Michael Jackson of KABC-Radio (an older white man)—Kennedy thought he was speaking to the singer Michael Jackson

On Ted Kennedy's Eloquent Opinion of Clinton Court Appointments

There are a number of, more even as the, Bill Rehnquist, who, the Supreme Court pointed that out.

Ted Kennedy responding to a question on Clinton's appointments, on Meet the Press

On the KGB, Open and Aboveboard

Only enemies of the Soviet Union can think of the KGB as some sort of secret police.

Yuri Andropov, then head of the KGB

On Kinder, Gentler Thoughts, Presidential

There are always going to be people who want to be president, and some days I'd like to give it to them.

President Bill Clinton

On Knowing, Socratic Ideas About

I know what I know is what he knows. . . . I don't know that I know everything.

George Bush on the Iran-Contra affair and Reagan

On Kuwait, Handy Hints for Postwar Belt-Tightening In

Instead [of having] four maids or three maids in the house, you can have two maids.

Abdel Rahman al-Awadi, Kuwaiti state minister for cabinet affairs

On Angela Lansbury, Dangerous

Why are they always blaming everything on the rappers? Don't blame the youth. Blame the wicked culture. Every Sunday night on TV, Angela Lansbury taught these kids violence on *Murder, She Wrote* . . . blame the reruns of *Have Gun Will Travel* and *Gunsmoke.*

the Reverend Al Sharpton when asked about the media coverage of the late gangsta rapper the Notorious B.I.G.

On Latin America, Shocking Discoveries About

I didn't go down there with any plans for the Americas, or anything. I went down there to find out from them and their views. You'd be surprised. They're all individual countries.

President Ronald Reagan to reporters after a five-day trip to Latin America

On Legal Defenses, Stretchy

Hear about the woman in South Carolina who drove her children into the river and drowned them? Mike Tyson didn't do that. . . . Hear about the bomb that was dropped on the building in Oklahoma City? Mike Tyson didn't do that. Do you all remember Jeffrey Dahmer, who ate all the people and put them in a refrigerator? Mike Tyson didn't do that.

C. Vernon Mason, political activist and attorney, in his defense argument for Mike Tyson after he was released from prison

On Legal Minds, Great

I always wait until a jury has spoken before I anticipate what they will do.

U.S. Attorney General Janet Reno

On Legislative Debate, Bizarre Moments In

I rise to object to the bill and especially to the amendment. . . . The one that failed. I didn't get to argue against it.

Representative D. A. "Butch" Gautreaux (D, Morgan City) during debate in the Louisiana state legislature

On Legislative Hairsplitting, Inadvertently Honest

This amendment does more damage than it does harm.

Representative Cynthia Willard-Lewis (D, New Orleans) during the 1996 Louisiana legislative session

On Legs, Armed

The advent of these sleek coaches should provide a shot in the arm to both legs of Nevada's passenger train system.

Senator Howard Cannon (D, Nev.)

On Letters Al Gore Probably Shouldn't Have Bothered to Send

To win in 2000, I need you by my side.

direct-mail letter sent by Democratic presidential candidate Al Gore to Republican presidential candidate and Texas governor George Bush

On Lies

We lie by not telling you things. . . . We don't lie by telling you things that aren't true.

unnamed U.S. official quoted in Newsday

On Life, Interesting Ways to Sanctify

Capital punishment is our society's recognition of the sanctity of human life.

Senator Orrin Hatch (R, Utah)

On Lifeboats, Flying

You get in the only available lifeboat and stay aloft.

Senator John Warner (R, Va.)

On Literary Questions, Despot-Style

Is death male or female? God only knows.

Libyan leader Muammar el-Qaddafi in his book Escape to Hell and Other Stories

On a Little Understanding, War Criminals And

Quite often . . . these little guys, who might be making atomic weapons or who might be guilty of some human rights violations or whatever, are looking for someone to listen to their problems and help them communicate.

Jimmy Carter explaining why he travels the world talking to dictators

On Lobbyists, Typical

They collected the money voluntarily and gave it to me with no strings attached.

Kim Hyun Chul, son of and adviser to Korean president Kim Young Sam, denying that the $3.6 million he got from businessmen had anything to do with trying to get him to influence his father

On Logic, Congressional

A species goes out of existence every twenty seconds. Surely a new species must come into existence every twenty seconds.

Idaho representative Helen Chenoweth in a House Resources Committee hearing on proposed drastic changes to the Endangered Species Act

On Looking at the Bright Side

I've spoken about a number of career opportunities, and one I've got to put in the blend is a prison ministry.

U.S. representative and evangelist Patrick Swindell (R, Ga.) after his conviction for perjury

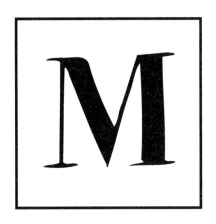

On Making Discrimination Available

[I favor] access to discrimination on the basis of sexual orientation.
Senator Ted Kennedy (D, Mass.)

On Making It Clear, Not Really

But that I'm out of touch with the American people, that I don't know people are hurting, I know it. I feel it. We pray about it, and I mean that literally at night, and, uh, many things, the various, where I don't care about, I don't know about education or don't, I mean, we've got a sound approach, innovative, revolutionary approach, and so I have to make it that clear.
President George Bush

On Making Things Perfectly Clear

New Orleans mayor Vic Schiro:

If you need me I'll be at hurricane headquarters.

Reporter:

Where is that, Mr. Mayor?

Schiro:

Wherever I am.

On Making Tough Decisions, Presidential Candidate Bob Dole And

Reporter:

Will you be rooting for the American League or National League in the All-Star Game?

Bob Dole:

Probably.

On Man's Best Friend

It has been said by some cynic, maybe it was a former president, "If you want a friend in Washington, get a dog." Well, we took them literally—that advice, as you know. But I didn't need that because I have Barbara Bush.

President George Bush

On the Marines, Amazing Insights About

There's a lot of good stuff [about the marines], but at the same time the purpose is war. It's a shame such a great organization has such a low purpose.

marine officer candidate Mary Brutzman of Charlotte, North Carolina

On Meat Eating, Greatness And

In the whole history of the world, whenever a meat-eating race has gone to war against a non-meat-eating race, the meat eaters won. It produces superior people. We have the books of history.

Senator Carl Curtis (R, Nebr.) during a debate on banning DES as a food additive for livestock

On Mediocrity

Even if he were mediocre, there are a lot of mediocre judges and people and lawyers. Don't *they* deserve some representation on the court?

Roman Hruska, Republican senator from Nebraska, defending Judge Harold Carswell, the first Nixon nominee for the Supreme Court, against charges that he was mediocre

On the Melting Pot, Frozen, Part 1

America must be kept American. Biological laws show . . . that Nordics deteriorate when mixed with other races.

President Calvin Coolidge

On the Melting Pot, Frozen, Part 2

Why are we more shocked when a dozen people are killed in Vilnius than by a massacre in Burundi? Because they are white people. That's who we are. That's where America comes from.

presidential candidate and columnist Pat Buchanan

On the Melting Pot, Very Hot

We are the boiling pot. We have open arms.

Senator Bob Dole attempting to discuss the nation's diversity—the melting pot

The Best Political False-Memory Syndrome

Many politicians seem to suffer from a strange affliction: the false-memory syndrome. They concoct false but quite diverting memories of their pasts—heroic log-splitting days that never were or inspiring moments that apparently happened in utero (not to mention the ever-popular saving orphans, slaying dragons . . . or commies . . . or mobsters . . . or drug dealers).

On Senators' Sons, Typical Days Of

[My father] taught me how to clean out hog waste with a shovel and a hose. He taught me how to clear land with an ax. He taught me how to plow a steep hillside with a team of mules. He taught me how to take up hay all day long in the hot sun and then, after a dinner break, go help the neighbors take up hay before the rain came and spoiled it on the ground.

Vice President Al Gore Jr. on the virtues of farm life, not mentioning that, as a rich senator's son, all this was presumably learned on summer vacation from Harvard. A real farmer's son, Republican National chairman Jim Nicholson, replied, "Mr. Vice President, with all due respect, you're shoveling a lot more of it right now than you ever did back then."

On Memories, Great Artificial Congressional

It is among the first memories I have of government of the United States, and probably the first hearing of the United States Senate I ever witnessed. It was only a flickering television screen, but I will never forget it, and even if I tried, my family would never allow me.

Senator Robert "Bob" Torricelli (D, N.J.) on the Senate hearings on organized crime in 1951, before he was born . . . meaning that he presumably watched the proceedings as a fetus or fertilized egg

On Memos, Urgent

Due to an error in numbering, Administrative Bulletin 94-05, addressed to all headquarters employees and concerning Holiday Season Security, should be renumbered to 94-07.

memo from the director of administration, National Labor Relations Board

On Memos from Your Senator, Very Urgent

Please be advised that whenever the Senator arrives by airplane to a media event taking place at the airport, there should be an official greeting party. As soon as the plane lands and comes to a complete stop, this greeting party should approach the plane and form a receiving line. In the past, the Senator has deboarded for a media event without a greeting party there to welcome him. There were TV cameras present to film the Senator having to walk to locate the people to meet, rather than having them walk to meet him. Obviously, we wish to avoid this situation in the future.

Senator Phil Gramm staffer Jeb Hensarling

On Men, What They <u>Must</u> Do

[Men] are biologically driven to go out and hunt giraffes.

Newt Gingrich, in a lecture titled "Renewing American Civilization"

On Metaphors, a Bit Odd

We gotta tighten up our bootstraps.

New Orleans mayor Vic Schiro

On Metaphors, a Little Confusing

I said last week that I was trying to keep a lid on my powder, but now it is time to fight fire with fire.

Senator Robert Packwood (R, Oreg.) attempting to explain why he was attacking the testimony of the seventeen women he was accused of sexually harassing

On Metaphors, a Little Confusing

He is trying to go around the bush to put out the fire.

witness during a Louisiana state legislature committee hearing, critiquing the sponsor of a bill

On Metaphors, Very Badly Mixed

I wanted to have all my ducks in a row so that if we did get into a posture, we could pretty much slam-dunk this thing and put it to bed.

Mayor Lee Cooke of Austin, Texas

On Middle Class, New Political Definitions Of

When I see someone who is making anywhere from $300,000 to $750,000, that's middle class.

Representative Frederick Heineman (R, N.C.) explaining why his then-income of $183,500 didn't make him rich enough to be considered middle class

On the Mideast Crisis

Why can't the Jews and the Arabs just sit down together and settle this like good Christians?

an unnamed senator

On Mideast Diplomacy, Great Moments In

President Gerald Ford, lifting his glass in a toast, at a state dinner given by Egyptian president Anwar Sadat:

[Here's to] the great people of the government of Israel . . . *Egypt,* excuse me.

On Minds, the Importance Of

What a waste it is to lose one's mind—or not to have a mind. How true that is.

Vice President Dan Quayle addressing a United Negro College Fund affair and garbling their slogan, "A mind is a terrible thing to waste."

On Minds, No Need For

This is still the greatest country in the world, if we just steel our wills and lose our minds.

President Bill Clinton

On the Missing Eighteen Minutes on the Watergate Tapes, One Man's Explanation

Oh, that was just an accident that happened.

President Richard Nixon

On Misspeaking

Then I misquoted, then I misspoke myself. I'm still exploring.
Governor George W. Bush clarifying a story suggesting that he had decided to run for president

On Mixed la Metaphors

We'll be giving them carte la blanche.
Eugene Whelan, then Canada's Liberal minister of agriculture—and famed for his malapropisms

On Mixed Metaphors

The defense budget is more than a piggy bank for people who want to get busy beating swords into plowshares.
President George Bush

On Mixed Metaphors

This has all the earmarks of an eyesore.
James McSheehy, member of the San Francisco Board of Supervisors, commenting on a construction project he was against

On Mixed Metaphors, Cutting

We have to belly up to the buzz saw, and I think we're reaping the whirlwind from it.

Senator Jim Sasser (D, Tenn.)

On Modern World War II Education, Orwellian Moments In

It was quite sexist in the war.

British government video for elementary schools issued in 1995 with a "modern" look at World War II

On Modes, Presidential

There are various groups that think you can ban certain kinds of guns. And I am not in that mode. I am in the mode of being deeply concerned.

President George Bush on assault rifles

On Money, Political Insights On

The public senses that $4.5 million is a lot of money.

Senator Bob Dole talking about his book contract

On Moral Standards, the Highest

You [Clinton] have demonstrated . . . a higher commitment to the kind of moral leadership that I value in public service and public policy than any person I have ever met.

Democratic national chairman Steve Grossman at a New York fund-raiser

On Moving Descriptions

The anguish, disbelief, and whatnot on my face, when he told me I was indictable.

John Ehrlichman

On Mummies, Enticing

You know, if I were a single man, I might ask that mummy out. That's a good-looking mummy!

President Bill Clinton looking at the recently discovered Inca mummy "Juanita"

On Mummies, Why They're Enticing

Probably she *does* look good compared to the mummy he's been fucking.

White House press secretary Mike McCurry in an off-the-cuff joke to reporters on the press plane

On Murder, Pithy Mayoral Thoughts About

I'm not going to let murder be the gauge [of police effectiveness], since we're not responsible for murder, can't stop the murders.

Marion Barry, former mayor of Washington, D.C.

On Mussels

Are these what regular people call clams?

Representative Roy Brun (R, Shreveport) during a Louisiana state legislature hearing on regulating freshwater mussels

On Name Changes in Support of Transportation Goals

Old name:

    Richard T. Pisani

New name:

    Richard Thomas Bullet Train Pisani

    Democratic candidate for lieutenant governor in Missouri, who officially changed his name for the greater transportation good of our country

On Names, True-Blue American

Wouldn't you like to have somebody named O'Reilly? . . . You know, so far we haven't found an American name.

H. Ross Perot on the number of "foreign," particularly Asian, names on the list of Clinton's campaign contributors—ignoring certain basic facts about the origins of 99 percent of Americans

On Nature

You can't just let nature run wild.

Walter Hickel, governor of Alaska, explaining why he wanted state officials to kill hundreds of wolves

On Naughtiness

How can we ever convince young people that it is wrong, that it is naughty, to smoke marijuana cigarettes?

Representative Bob Dornan (R, Calif.)

On Needs, Modest

People say, "Mrs. Marcos, you are lavish, you are excessive." . . . I don't know how to explain it, but there is really nothing I want for myself, nothing.

Imelda Marcos, first lady of the Philippines and owner of many shoes

On New Adverbs

We don't believe in denominationally moving in.

George Bush clarifying his position on the relationship between church and state during the 1984 vice-presidential debates

On New Coliseums, Teensy-Weensy Economic Value Of

[It] is an asset of infinitesimal value to the vitality and growth of our city.

Cincinnati mayor Theodore M. Berry commenting on the new Riverfront Coliseum, as reported in the Cincinnati Enquirer

On New Legislation, Dubious

One important new area is proposed legislation to promote unfair discrimination against people with disabilities.

from Great Britain's Forward Look of Government-funded Science, Engineering and Technology

On New York Mayors, a Little Too Present

I'm here! It's me! It's Mayor Koch! I'm here!

New York mayor Ed Koch announcing his presence to East German guards at the Berlin Wall

On New York Senators, Sexy Endorsements From

I hope she will go all the way. I mean to go all the way with her.
Senator Daniel Patrick Moynihan (D, N.Y.) backing Hillary Clinton's bid for his seat

On Non-PC Poles

Women are to have fun with. In politics, I prefer not to see a woman. Instead of getting all worked up, they should stay as they are—like flowers.
Polish leader Lech Walesa (Interestingly, ten years later, his prime minister—a woman named Hanna Suchoka—was instrumental in revitalizing the Polish economy.)

On Non-PC Problems

First they tax our beer, then they tax cigarettes. Now they are going to increase the tax on gasoline. All that's left are our women.
Senator John East (R, N.C.)

On Nouns, Catchy

I resent your insinuendoes.
Chicago mayor Richard J. Daley

On Nouns, New Republican

The more we remove penalties for being a bum, the more bumism is going to blossom.
Senator Jesse Helms commenting against welfare

On Nowness, Ultimate Thoughts About

Things are more like they are now than they have ever been.
President Gerald Ford

On Nuclear Attacks, IRS Role In

During state of national emergency resulting from enemy attack, the essential functions of the Service will be as follows: (1) assessing, collecting, and recording taxes. . . .

Internal Revenue Service Handbook, *1976*

The Politicians Most Able to Look at Life from Both Sides Now

The ideal politician, of course, is one who pleases all his constituents all of the time. Yes, this is impossible in *fact*, but happily, not in theory. And all good politicians are fascinated by theory, since so few of them, as angry businesspeople are wont to say, have ever met a payroll.

Thus we find many politicians who opt for the theoretical and make supremely confident diametrical assertions on both sides (or even on several sides) of an issue. We cannot but admire such astute readers of the electorate, who most certainly recognize the diverse opinions of the public and go out of their way to assert to their diverse constituents that their diverse views, whatever they may be, are absolutely correct.

Here forthwith are two examples from some modern, shall we say, *multifaceted* politicians.

On Integrity, Senatorial

Thank you for contacting me to express your opposition . . . to the early use of military by the U.S. against Iraq. I share your concerns. On January 11, I voted in favor of a resolution that would have insisted that economic sanctions be given more time to work and against a resolution giving the president the immediate authority to go to war.

January 22, 1991, letter from Senator John Kerry (D, Mass.) to a constituent

Thank you for contacting me to express your support for the actions of President Bush in response to the Iraqi invasion of Kuwait. From the outset of the invasion, I have strongly and unequivocally supported President Bush's response to the crises and the policy goals he has established with our military deployment in the Persian Gulf.

January 31, 1991, letter from Senator John Kerry to the same *constituent*

On Congresspersons, New Touchy-Feely

Congressman Bill Young's speech in Congress:

The B-52 has been an effective war machine. It's killed a lot of people.

Congressman Bill Young's speech as officially recorded in the Congressional Record—*after staffers complained that he sounded too warlike:*

The B-52 has been an effective war machine, which has unfortunately killed a lot of people.

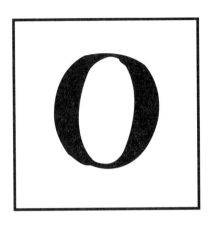

On Observations Some Other Presidents Might Agree With

When the president does it, that means it's not illegal.

President Richard Nixon in 1974, just before the nation begged to differ

On Old Chinese Sayings

Hey, listen. I'm a member of the NRA. You're hurting my feelings, as they say in China.

President George Bush explaining why he didn't come out strongly against violence against women in an address to the National Rifle Association

On Old Sayings, New Twists On

Let's get that in black and writing.

attributed to Slaw Rebchuck, Winnipeg (Canada) councilman, during a city council meeting

On Ontario, Great Equal Rights Moments In

We'd like to pay her the same as the men get, but times are tough.

Ontario Premier William Davis explaining why Education Minister Bette Stephenson's salary had to be cut by 35 percent

On Open Government, True Moments With

State Department spokesperson Bernard Kalb:

[I'm making it my New Year's resolution to be] candid, frank, useful, and constructive.

Answering first question from reporter:

I have nothing that I can offer you on that.

On Open Minds, Presidential

I believe that this country's policies should be heavily biased in favor of nondiscrimination.

President Bill Clinton

On Opening Up Nations to Democracy, Democratic Thoughts About

I intend to open this country up to democracy, and anyone who is against that, I will jail, I will crush.

General João Baptista Figueiredo upon becoming president of Brazil

On Opinions, Opinionated

. . . she's a damn lesbian. I'm not going to put a damn lesbian in a position like that. If you want to call me a bigot, fine.

Senator Jesse Helms (R, N.C.) on the appointment of Roberta Achtenburg as assistant secretary in the Department of Housing and Urban Development

On Opinions, Strong

I have opinions of my own—strong opinions—but I don't always agree with them.

President George Bush

On Opinions, Strong

Basically, [I'm] a dog person. I wouldn't want to offend my constituents who are cat people, and I should say that being, I hope, a sensitive person, that I have nothing against cats, and had cats when I was a boy, and if we didn't have two dogs might very well be interested in having a cat now.

Missouri congressman James Talent when asked by a reporter if he were a dog or a cat person

On Oral Tests, Need for Pencil For

The Department of Employee Relations reserves the right to call only the most qualified candidates to oral and performance examinations. Oral examinations may include written exercises . . .

employment listing by the City of Milwaukee

On Ordinary Americans, What the President Thinks About

We can't be so fixated on our desire to preserve the rights of ordinary Americans. . . .

President Bill Clinton talking about his opposition to the NRA

On the Oval Office, Press Secretarial Lack of Knowledge Of

Because there is no privacy, there is no way to do it if you wanted to.

Mike McCurry, Clinton press secretary, commenting on allegations of sexual encounters in the Oval Office

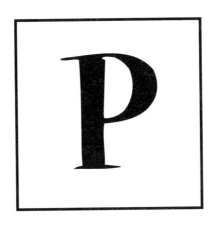

On Paranoia, Third-Party Candidates And

[They say] Perot never threw a paper route on a horse in a black neighborhood. I can produce people from the neighborhood. I can produce numerous witnesses. I did it. They just run these off stories.

Ross Perot on NBC's Meet the Press

On Pentagon Briefings, Informative

Reporter:

How many NATO strikes have been aborted due to bad weather?

Vice Admiral Scott Fry:

I'm afraid I can't get into that level of detail right off the top of my head.

Reporter:

How about an approximation?

Vice Admiral Scott Fry:

I'd prefer not to even approximate it.

Reporter:

How about a ballpark figure?

Vice Admiral Scott Fry:

I don't have that information available.

Reporter:

How many of [Yugoslavian President] Milosevic's surface-to-air-missile launchers have been taken out by NATO?

Vice Admiral Scott Fry:

That's a military number I'm not going to talk about.

Reporter:

How about a guess?

Vice Admiral Scott Fry:

A large percentage.

Reporter:

A large percentage of the missile launchers?

Vice Admiral Scott Fry:
    The launchers themselves, no.
    Pentagon briefing on the Kosovo war

On Percentages, a Little Confusing
    The brave men who died in Vietnam, more than one hundred percent of which were black, were the ultimate sacrifice.
    Marion Barry, mayor of Washington, D.C.

On Personal Responsibility, Great Presidential Moments
President Bill Clinton in January 1997:
    Each and every one of us, in our own way, must assume personal responsibility not only for ourselves and our families, but for our neighbors and our nation.
Clinton in January 1998:
    I want to say one thing to the American people. I want you to listen to me. I'm going to say this again: I did not have sexual relations with that woman, Miss Lewinsky.
Clinton in July 1998:
    I did have a relationship with Miss Lewinsky that was not appropriate. In fact, it was wrong . . .

On Pesticides, New Uses For

Are they taking DDT?

Vice President Dan Quayle asking doctors at a Manhattan AIDS clinic about their treatments of choice—and meaning to refer to AZT

On Phi Beta Klan

There are different Klans—just like there's different fraternities at college.

Republican congressional candidate David Duke of Louisiana talking about his former membership in the Ku Klux Klan

On Plane Crashes, Why They Happen

Affirmative action programs.

David Duke in a 1996 political debate when running for the Senate and explaining the real reasons behind the TWA and Valujet air crashes that had recently occurred (note: he came in fourth in Louisiana's GOP primary)

On Poesy, Politically Incorrect

Oh, what a tangled web we have, when first we practice to deceive.

congressman garbling the famous line during a conversation about the Clinton impeachment trial on NBC's Meet the Press, *February 7, 1999*

On Points, Ever So Illuminating

Now, the only thing that remains unresolved is the resolution of the problem.

Thomas Wells, minister of education, in the Ontario legislature

On Police

Get the thing straight once and for all. The policeman isn't there to create disorder. The policeman is there to preserve disorder.

Richard J. Daley, mayor of Chicago

On Political Ads, Somewhat . . . Um . . . Different

Desperately Seeking to Be Your State Senator

My name is Michael and I am running for state senate, Senate District 65. I am a conservative, God-fearing, moral, pro-life Republican. I am also seeking a faithful, devoted, obedient, God-fearing woman to be my wife, to share my life, & to bear my children. Please respond by letter with picture. Campaign donations may be sent to this Meet People box # . . .

ad placed in the personals section of the paper by Mike Gubash when running for a seat in the Minnesota Senate. Sadly, the innovative advertising concept failed. Explaining that he got no responses whatsoever, Gubash explained, "I don't know if it's just me or if women don't want a man who's assertive."

On Political Arguments, Appalling

Why in God's name we're going to punish a man for having sex with his wife when she says, "No, not tonight," I don't know.

Bud Long, state senator from South Carolina, opposing a spousal rape law

On Political Candidates, in Touch with Their Children

Q:

Where do your children go to school?

Michael Huffington, then Senate candidate from California:

Saint, Saint . . . Saint something or other. Ask my wife. She'll know.

On Political Candidates, in Touch with Their Feelings

I do believe in smelling the flowers. Occasionally, I will take my staff out to the lawn out there and sit there and say, "Look at this Capitol, look at these trees. Smell it."

Michael Huffington, who spent $28 million in an attempt to win a U.S. Senate seat from California

On Political Comments, Classy

Why you got your boob covered up?

Representative Ernest Konnyu (R, Calif.) to a female aide

On Political Comments, Classy Explanations Of

She wore her name tag right over her boobs. . . . I don't think it was right for her to have her name tag on in a—it should be up high. She's not exactly heavily stacked, okay? . . . So I told her . . . to move the darn name tag off her boobs.

Representative Ernest Konnyu trying later to explain away his comment

On Political Counting

Remember, there's only one taxpayer—you and me.
attributed to Calgary councilman John Kushner

On Political Defenses, Not That Great

There are a thousand things, not including sex, which could have gone on, which fall well short of adultery. . . . Let's assume that some of the allegations that Hillary sometimes—not necessarily being into regular sex with men—might be true. Let's assume that this is a guy who has been sexually active for a long time and then got it that as president . . . he'd have to shut himself down. You would then expect a variety of things which would be quasi-sexual in nature but which would fall short of it. . . . Phone sex might be one of them, fantasies might be one of them. . . . Those all could be real things without actually committing adultery.

Dick Morris, presidential adviser to Bill Clinton—and also star of his own sex scandal, which involved a toe-sucking call girl

On Political Discourse, Dubious

[My opponent doesn't have] a hope in hell because of her three bastard children.

British Tory MP David Evans about his Labour opponent, Melanie Johnson

On Political Discrimination, Harrowing Moments In

How come *I* never get any plums—or apples or peaches or pears?

attributed to Slaw Rebchuck, Winnipeg (Canada) councilman, during a city council meeting

The Lamest Political Excuses

"The buck stops here," good ol' Harry Truman said. Our modern politician will heartily agree, but then quickly point out that, in his or her case, the buck should actually keep going . . . right down over there.

After all, Teflon and the presidency have been synonymous since the Reagan years. We have now grown accustomed to seeing politicians of all stripes deftly deflecting blame with carefully executed excuses designed to let it all slide right off.

However, to paraphrase another famous president, not all excuses are created equal. So often we find politicians making excuses that act more like Velcro than Teflon—making matters stickier than ever.

On Bouncing Eighty-One Checks, Great Statements About

It's not like molesting young girls or young boys. It's not a show-stopper.

Representative Charlie Wilson (Texas) on his bouncing eighty-one checks at the House of Representatives bank

On Excuses, Excuses

Bill Clinton (in a taped phone conversation with Gennifer Flowers):

[Mario Cuomo is a] mean son of a bitch who acts like a mafioso.

Bill Clinton (later explaining his statement):

If the remarks on the tape left anyone with the impression that I was disrespectful to either Governor Cuomo or Italian-Americans, then I deeply regret it.

On Explanations, Enlightening

First, it was not a strip bar, it was an erotic club. And second, what can I say? I'm a night owl.

Marion Barry, mayor of Washington, D.C.

On Political Ethics Laws, Huge Problems With

Our system has gone too far. . . . If you breakfast with someone and have a coffee and rolls, that is okay. But if you have a *croissant,* that is over the rule.

Heather Foley, wife and chief political adviser of former Speaker of the House and U.S. ambassador to Japan Thomas Foley, at a Japan Press Club appearance (just as the Japanese were considering ethics legislation of their own—something the U.S. government had been lobbying hard for)

On Political Explanations, Zingy

They see these things they believed in for so long happening overnight—zing, zing, zing, balanced-budget amendment, line-item veto—and everything swish, swish, swish. . . . It isn't something where the Speaker says, "We'll finish this tonight, zing, zing."

Senator John Chafee (R, Rhode Island) on the not-so-zingy pace of Senate life as perceived by whooshing House members

On Political Hypocrisy, Great Moments In

I think it is a shoddy, unusual thing to use the floor of the Senate to attack your opponent without any proof whatsoever.

Senator Joe McCarthy, famed for his Senate hearings in which he claimed numerous people were Communists—with no proof

On Political Imagery, Evocative

We want a prisoner to look like a prisoner, to smell like a prisoner. . . . When you see one of those boogers aloose, you'll say, "I didn't know we had zebras in Mississippi."

Mississippi state representative Mack McInnis (Lucedale), after a vote passed in the statehouse to put prisoners in high-visibility, reflective, zebra-striped uniforms

On Political Indecent Exposure, Why Not to Worry About

The people here have known me all my life. They know I've had a few problems, [but] they know I love this town.

Spencer Schlosnagel, mayor of Friendsville, Maryland, explaining why he wasn't planning to resign from his post even though he had been repeatedly convicted for indecent exposure, as quoted in the Chicago Tribune

On Political Integrity, Great Moments In

I'm not going to come out with programs that will defeat me, no matter how I stand on that program, because I want to get elected. There may be some programs that you believe in and I believe in that will not be campaign issues, because if they are, I won't be governor.

Robert B. Jordan III, lieutenant governor of North Carolina, when campaigning for the Democratic gubernatorial nomination

On Political Letters, No Comment Department

J. A. Cartrette Construction Co.

Dear Governor Hunt,

I have waited to write to see your decision about the DOT and Wildlife appointments. We have never had anything like this happen before.

Attached is a copy of a letter that was mailed to Jim Bennett. It explains what happened and the promise you, Garland, and Jim made. Jim told us several times that Allen would get the Wildlife appointment and I would get the DOT appointment. Jim denies this, but this promise was made to three (3) of us. I understand that Mr. R. C. Soles Jr. stopped these appointments. When I read in the Wilmington paper that Michael Mills was going to the DOT, I lost all confidence in the system.

Each of you misrepresented the truth to us. We gave money and would have given more if you would have asked. We gave you the money and have supported you all through your career. We are very disappointed and feel that our money should be returned.

Sincerely,
J. A. Cartrette

On Political Memory, Convenient

Q:

And are you presently still an officer or director of [Albo]?

Representative Tom DeLay:

I don't think so. No.

Q:

All right, you're still an officer, are you not?

DeLay:

I don't think I am.

Q:

Okay. Did you resign as an officer?

DeLay:

Not written. It was sort of an agreement. . . .

[In later testimony]: I'm not even sure I am resigned. . . . I have nothing to do with the company. And in the day-to-day operations of the company.

Representative Tom DeLay (R, Tex.) testifying in a lawsuit that charged that he and an associate used money from Albo (a company) to pay off campaign loans and more

On Political Metaphors, Confusing Simian

Jimmy Long says that if you get fifty-three votes for this one, then you could get a monkey to eat red pepper and watch him jump. If you can't get fifty-three votes, then you go to burying that monkey where nobody can see him.

Louisiana state representative Charles DeWitt (D, Lacompte) during legislative debate

On Political Moments, Hair-Raising

Well, don't get your dandruff up.
attributed to Calgary councilman John Kushner

On Political Newspaper Corrections, Essential

A news analysis article on Saturday about the politics behind Governor Pete Wilson's role in eliminating affirmative action programs at University of California campuses rendered a word incorrectly in a quotation from Sherry Bebitch Jeffe, a former legislative aide in Sacramento. Ms. Jeffe said of Mr. Wilson: "He's been biding his time on this knowing all along what he was going to do when the time was ripe. It's ripe. He's picked."

She did not say, "He's pickled."
correction in The New York Times

On Political Poems, Putrid

We have hobby, it's called "breeding,"
Welfare pays for baby feeding.
Kids need dentist? Wife need pills?
We get free, we got no bills.
We think America damn good place,
Too damn good for white man's race.
If they no like us, they can go,
Got lots of room in Mexico.
poem by California state assemblyman William J. Knight, which he gave to fellow Assembly members

On Political Promises, New Twists On

[I endorse] the right to be dumb, ugly, and rich.
platform of independent candidate Jacob Haugaard, a musician, comedian, and actor who ran for—and won—a seat on the Danish parliament; he later said, "It's incredible that I got elected on this twaddle."

On Political Stances, Weird

Sometimes in order to make progress and move ahead, you have to stand up and do the wrong thing.
Representative Gary Ackerman (D, N.Y.) explaining why he supported the new welfare bill

On Political Stances That Don't Win Elections

I hope I stand for antibigotry, anti-Semitism, antiracism. This is what drives me.

George Bush in 1988 when aides accused of anti-Semitism resigned from his campaign

On Political Statements, Enigmatic

I wish Mr. Copelin's plan was side by mine.

Representative Francis Thompson (D, Delhi) during a Louisiana state legislature meeting

On Political Truths

I don't see why the legislature should be in the business of artificial intelligence, real intelligence or any intelligence at all.

Louisiana House Speaker Hunt Downer (D, Houma) commenting on a budget request for computer software

On Political Wisdom, Outrageous

The facts show that people who are raped—who are truly raped—the juices don't flow, the body functions don't work, and they don't get pregnant.

Henry Aldridge, Republican state representative of North Carolina, explaining his support for a bill eliminating the state abortion fund for poor women

On Politically Correct Clichés

These are times that try men's souls and women's souls.

Senator Don Riegle (D, Mich.)

On Politically Correct Moments, Congressional

There are some who say there are so many women now on the floor of Congress, it looks like a mall.

Representative Henry Hyde (R, Ill.)

On Politically Incorrect Moments

The warm-climate community just hasn't found the colder climate that attractive. It's an area of America that simply has never attracted the Afro-American or the Hispanic.

Representative Helen Chenoweth (R, Idaho) explaining why she believed that the U.S. Forest Service shouldn't try to recruit minority members for service in Idaho

On Politicians, Ethical Standards For

To forcibly remove a politician from public office, one has to meet a much higher standard of dishonesty.

Santa Barbara attorney Michael Coney replying to people who wanted to oust a city councilman who had switched price tags on items he was going to buy in a store

On Politicians, Not Dead

I don't know anyone here that's been killed with a handgun.

Representative Avery Alexander (D, New Orleans), Louisiana legislature, during a debate on gun control

On Politicians, Opinionated

Don't quote me as saying that we will or we should increase our external aid. That would be my opinion if I had an opinion, but as a member of my government, I have no opinion.

Canadian external affairs minister Paul Martin in response to a question by the Toronto press

On Pollution, What It Really Is

It isn't pollution that's harming our environment. It's the impurities in our air and water that are doing it.

Vice President Dan Quayle

On Pompous Reasons to Cut in Front of Other People

I'm terribly sorry, but would you mind if my wife and I butted in? The thing is, I've got to go and see the queen at six o'clock.

British prime minister Tony Blair to other parents waiting in line for their parent-teacher conference at the school that Blair's children attend

On the Pot Calling . . .

I hate it when people blame someone else and don't take responsibility.

President Bill Clinton discussing with Virginia students the problems he sees with American youth that may have led to the high school shootings in Littleton, Colorado

On Praise, Overbearing

I would like to praise Mr. Debs for the dogmatic way he pursued this subject.

Frank G. Bonelli, Los Angeles County Board of Supervisors, attempting to congratulate his fellow supervisor for a job well done

On Praising with Faint Praise

Reporter:

[Could you say anything positive about your opponent, Mary Landrieu?]

Candidate for U.S. senator from Louisiana Woody Jenkins (R):

She's attractive. . . . I love New Orleans. She's from New Orleans and that's good.

Asked the same question, Mary Landrieu (D) said:

"He's a smooth talker."

On Predictions, Pretty Bad

No woman in my time will be prime minister or chancellor or foreign secretary—not the top jobs. Anyway, I wouldn't want to be prime minister. You have to give yourself one hundred percent.

Margaret Thatcher, then "shadow spokesman on education," in 1969—ten years before she became the first female prime minister of England

On the Present, Problem With

Today the real problem is the future.

Richard J. Daley, mayor of Chicago

On Presidential Campaigns, What's Really Important In

Reporter:

What will you be telling voters during your heartland campaign tour?

Republican candidate Bob Dole:

We're trying to get good pictures. Don't worry very much about what I say.

On Presidential Candidates, Exciting

This is the first living-room conversation of the year 2000 campaign that I've had the privilege to engage in.

Al Gore during a New Hampshire campaign appearance

The Most Dexterous Political Hairsplitting

Ask a politician a pointed question and he or she often calls upon one of the most vital weapons in his or her verbal arsenal: the splitting of hairs.

If one can prove, through the miracle of modern etymology, that what one said didn't really mean what everyone else thinks it meant, then many a political gaffe can be avoided, as can all sorts of unpleasant things such as losing elections, being laughed at, and being convicted of perjury and contempt of court.

And so we are left with some fascinating examples of politicians researching the true, underlying meaning of words and actions, enough to make a grown philologist cry from sheer joy.

On Answers, Crystal Clear

Reporter:

[Did you attend the White House fund-raiser?]

Senator Chris Dodd (D, Conn.):

I would not argue I was there, and I would not argue that I was not there.

On Being Alone, Fascinating Presidential Discourses About

[I]t depends on how you define *alone* . . . there were a lot of times when we were alone, but I never really thought we were.

President Bill Clinton in his grand jury testimony about the Monica Lewinsky affair

On Lying, Other Words For

I made no attempt to be inaccurate, but I want to be clear I was not attempting to be precise.

Treasury chief of staff Josh Steiner, accused by Congress of lying when his diary entries did not jibe at all with what he told them

On Sleep, New Definitions Of

It's not true [the Congressman was sleeping during the debate]. He was just taking a few moments for deep reflection.

aide to Representative Martin Hoke (R, Ohio), seen on the House floor with his eyes closed during a debate on the Contract with America

On Testimony, Great Moments In

It depends on what the meaning of the word *is* is.
President Bill Clinton

On Presidential Lawyers, Great Legal Moments And

Clinton lawyer Bill Bennett defending the presidential organ on Meet the Press:

There is absolutely no unique characteristic of any kind . . . in terms of size, shape, direction. . . . The president is a normal man.

On Presidential Spokesmen, Great Answers From

Q:

Did the president misspeak when he talked about the Monica Lewinsky affair?

Joe Lockhart, acting spokesman:

There were several things in his mind that he was talking about.

Q:

But did he misspeak?

Lockhart:

If that was your interpretation of what he said, that was the wrong interpretation.

Joe Lockhart, acting press secretary while Mike McCurry was out of town, after the Monica Lewinsky affair first broke

On Presidents, Ones Who May Not Win the Female Vote

A woman's place is in the bedroom.

Ferdinand Marcos, Philippine president—who was ousted and replaced by a woman, Corazon Aquino

On Press Conferences, Openness At

That's a good question and let me state the problem more clearly without going too deeply into the answer.

National Security Chief Brent Scowcroft at a press briefing

On Press Relations

I'm not going to discuss what I'm going to bring up. . . . Even if I don't discuss it, I'm not going to discuss it.

President George Bush talking about his relationship with the press

On Press Relations, How Not to Have Good

Get that whore off my chair!

attributed to Senator Steve Simms (R, Idaho) when he spotted a female TV reporter—who had been critical of him on the air—sitting in his chair

On Press Secretaries, Confusing

If my answers sound confusing, I think they are confusing because the questions are confusing, and the situation is confusing and I'm not in a position to clarify it.

Ron Ziegler, Nixon press secretary

On Press Secretaries, Things They Probably Shouldn't Say to Female Reporters, Part 1

Who'd you sleep with to get your job?

Jon Peck, former press secretary to Bob Martinez, former governor of Florida, to a female reporter

On Press Secretaries, Things They Probably Shouldn't Say to Female Reporters, Part 2

If you took all off all your clothes and sat on my face, I might tell you.

Peter Freyne, former press secretary to the governor of Vermont, to a reporter

On Priorities, Scrooge-Like

You mention balancing the budget as though it were somehow less meritorious a case or goal than taking care of children.

Representative Henry Hyde (R, Ill.) as quoted in a newsletter for the American Academy of Pediatrics, explaining why he supported cuts in child-welfare programs

On Problems, Problem With

We'd like to avoid problems, because when we have problems, we can have troubles.

Arizona governor Wesley Bolin

On Problems, Problems, Problems

There's no doubt in my mind that he has a problem, or problems, and that he needs some help with those problems and that he ought to get some help with those problems, because you can't keep doing things like this and have that kind of reckless conduct without it being a very serious problem.

Senator Orrin Hatch (R, Utah) discussing Clinton's problems

On Procedure, Fascinating Senatorial Thoughts On

Comments from different senators on the first day of the Clinton impeachment trial, as reported in the New Republic:

We've got to get the ground rules hammered out and find a procedure.

Senator Ron Wyden (D, Oreg.)

[There is] no procedural agreement on the procedures.

Senator Bob Kerrey (D, Nebr.)

[We need] some kind of procedure.

Senator Frank Murkowski (R, Alaska)

If there's no ground rules, there is no procedure.
Senator Olympia Snowe (R, Maine)

We will proceed with rules.
Senator Trent Lott (R, Miss.)

On Pro-Choice Men, One Man's View

These are either women trapped in men's bodies, like Alan Alda or Phil Donahue, or younger guys who are like camp followers looking for easy sex.

Representative Bob Dornan (R, Calif.) talking about men who are pro-choice

On Promises, Absolute

Can I make the promise I won't support [new taxes]? Absolutely. But, you know, sometimes you run into new realities.

President George Bush when asked about his position on raising taxes

On Promises, Not So Pedestrian

I promise you a police car on every sidewalk.
Marion Barry, mayor of Washington, D.C.

On Promises, Promises

We should use the liberation of term limits to smash open our grid-locked yet out-of-control congress.

Marty Meehan (D, Mass.) when running for a congressional seat in 1992

I favor limiting members of congress to four terms, and I commit to serve no longer than that even if term-limit legislation is not enacted.

Marty Meehan spelling it out even more in a position paper he released while campaigning in 1992

I am obviously more effective today than I was when I arrived. My district would be better off with a member of congress who utilizes his or her seniority to take advantage of the district.

Representative Meehan, in 1999, now a four-term incumbent, explaining that term limits aren't all they're cracked up to be, and maintaining that not keeping an old promise can actually be a sign of "growth," even "independence"

It was a mistake to blurt out [the term-limits pledge].

Representative Meehan further trying to explain his new position to the Boston Herald

[The term limits pledge was] a youthful indiscretion.

Representative Meehan trying one more time, to the Lawrence Eagle-Tribune

On Property Rights, Dubious Explanations Of

When Lincoln freed the slaves, he did not pay for them.

Marshall Kuykendall, political activist and president of Take Back Texas, speaking at a property rights forum and explaining that the government takes property without compensating the original owner

On Proverbs, New

If you give a person a fish, they'll fish for a day. But if you train a person to fish, they'll fish for a lifetime.

Vice President Dan Quayle while at a job training center in Atlanta celebrating the tenth anniversary of the Job Training Partnership Act, which Quayle helped to sponsor while a senator

On Proverbs, New and Improved

Those who throw rocks in glass houses had better look at yourself.

Senator Dennis DeConcini (R, Ariz.) after the NFL had pulled the Super Bowl out of Arizona

On Prowess, Political

Some of his women complained. In my case, no one ever complained.

Philippine president Joseph "Erap" Estrada commenting on the differences between him and Bill Clinton

On Psychic Ability of Dan Quayle

I have made good judgments in the past. I have made good judgments in the future.

Dan Quayle in a Los Angeles Times *interview*

On the Public, CIA View Of

The press says that the public has a right to know everything. That's a load of garbage.

CIA spokesman George Lauder

On Putting Air Conditioners in the Prison Death Chamber, Good Reasons For

It makes it more comfortable for everybody.

Virginia Corrections Department official on decision to install a brand-new air-conditioning system in the execution room

On Putting It Nice and Clearly

To the extent that when one measures real interest rates by effectively subtracting the inflation rate from nominal interest rates, if there is a bias in the inflation rate and it hasn't changed very significantly, it means that the level of inflation that—once it subtracts from the nominal interest rate—is lower across the board of history, and that the real interest rate measured is correspondingly higher

Alan Greenspan, chairman of the Federal Reserve Board

On Qualifications for Holding Political Office

Anyone can be elected governor. I'm proof of that.
Joe Frank Harris, two-term Georgia governor, talking about who might fill his shoes

On the Queen of England, Star Quality Of

Queen Elizabeth Taylor.
Thai prime minister Banharn Silpa-archa, referring to the Queen of England

On Questions, Deep

Tell me, General, how dead is the Dead Sea?

President George Bush on a visit to Jordan. His host, General Zayid bin Shakr, answered, "Very dead, sir."

On Questions, Deeper

[The question] is too suppository.

Alexander Haig refusing to answer a question at a Senate committee hearing

On Questions, Good

What does an actor know about politics?

President Ronald Reagan complaining about Screen Actors Guild president Ed Asner's speaking out on U.S. foreign policy

On Questions, Stupid

Why would we have different races if God meant us to be alike and associate with each other?

Lester Maddox, former governor of Georgia

On Questions with Are Instead of Is, Prescient

I think it's a legitimate question: Are you now or recently have you been running around with a bunch of bimbos?

then presidential candidate Pat Robertson when rumors of Bill Clinton's first affair (the one with Gennifer Flowers) broke into the news

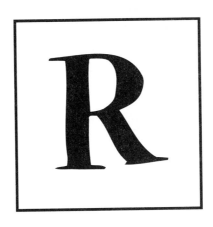

On Rallies, Precisely Spontaneous

The spontaneous rally will begin at 1:45.
Mike Murphy, adviser to Lamar Alexander in his bid for the Republican presidential nomination

On Ramifistations, Bad

It could have bad ramifistations in the hilterlands.
Gib Lewis, Speaker of the Texas House

On Reactions, A Little <u>Too</u> Colorful

I would kind of like to throw up in living color.

Representative Pat Schroeder (D, Colo.) reacting to the Clinton strategist Dick Morris sex scandal

On Reactions, A Little <u>Too</u> Well-Described for Our Tastes

I was awakened by the sounds of distress coming from the bathroom. Mother had lost her dinner.

Elizabeth "Liddy" Dole, Republican presidential candidate, describing how her mother reacted after Dole told her she was going to attend Harvard Law School

The Most Gripping Banalities

At a loss for profundity or unwilling to run the risk of taking a possibly unpopular stance, politicians often fall back into that easy chair of political commentary: the banality.

This is especially popular during speeches, when politicians can declaim at length about such noncontroversial topics as children (good) or wealth for all (also good) and, of course, the old-fashioned tautology— expounding on where the future is (in the future), etc., etc.

On the Future, Where to Find

The future's right in front of us.

Senator Bob Dole in a campaign speech

On Imports, Fascinating Facts About

Traditionally, most of Australia's imports come from overseas.

former Australian cabinet minister Keppel Enderbery

On Insights, Insightful

The first black president will be a politician who is black.

L. Douglas Wilder, governor of Virginia

On Reasons to Run for Office

The little people have needs.

Senator Al D'Amato (R, N.Y.)

On Reducing Energy Usage, Novel Ways

We should abolish January and February. If we then divided the fifty-nine extra days between July and August, we will cut our energy needs by about one-third through eliminating the coldest days of the year. Cold is largely a psychological matter. If people look at the calendar and see that it is July, they will be quite happy to turn the heat down.

state representative John Galbraith of Ohio

On Relax, It's Just a Theme Park Company

One story after another, whether it is taking that Italian classic, *Pinocchio*, or a British classic like *Peter Pan*, he took the past works, added to his own creations, and has given us a timeless legacy where, centuries from now when everybody is forgotten in this House—and I know the president would not mind my saying even Ronald Reagan retreating to a few paragraphs—they will be adding more stereophonic sound quality, more Dolby sound quality and more color enhancement and probably three dimensions to all of these works of Walt Disney. . . . Walt Disney Recognition Day. What a joy!

Congressman Bob Dornan (R, Calif.) on our important new national holiday: Walt Disney Recognition Day

On Religious Sincerity, Great Presidential Moments In

We wanted wall-to-wall coverage of the pope leaning against the president for help, of the pope thanking the president. The president isn't Catholic, but he can play like one on TV and look like one in the morning papers. That would have been the equivalent to being forgiven for his sins.

Clinton press aide expressing disappointment that the Vatican didn't allow for more press opportunities with Clinton during the pope's visit to the United States in 1999

On Repeat That Please

How many people are going to emulate now, trying to go to high school like Sharon Stone, with no underwear on because she uncrossed her legs in front of five detectives?

Representative Bob Dornan (R, Calif.)

On Repeat That Too, Please

Following a nuclear attack on the United States, the United States Postal Service plans to distribute Emergency Change of Address Cards.

U.S. Federal Emergency Management Agency Executive Order 11490

On Representatives, Alert

Louisiana state House Speaker John Alario (D, Westwego):

There is no objection to the motion to make Forster's bill special order of the day, Monday.

Representative Garey Forster:

Are we meeting on Monday?

On Representing All the People

Students don't vote. Do you expect me to come here and kiss your ass?
Georgia senator Wyche Fowler, to student-aged volunteers who were campaigning for deficit reductions (Fowler denies the comment, but the volunteers say he made it.)

On Republican National Committee, Great Thoughts Of

. . . when the local government becomes too close to the people it inevitably leads to corruption.
Republican National Committeeman Van H. Archer Jr. on his opposition to electing city council members from residential districts

On Republicans, Nose-Pleasing

They [the state Democrats, who were banning cologne or perfume at their convention] want to regulate people right down to how they smell. Our convention will have loud noises, bright lights, and sweet-smelling people.
Minnesota state Republican chief Tony Sutton commenting on news that state Democratic convention attendees were asked not to wear cologne or perfume in courtesy to fellow attendees who could "experience unpleasant reactions"

On Rises, Weighty

There is no question that the heavy part of our rise is behind us.
Secretary of Agriculture Earl Butz

On Pat Robertson, Time to Become a Feminist

The key in terms of mental [ability] is chess. There's never been a woman Grand Master chess player. Once you get one, then I'll buy some of the feminism.
periodic presidential candidate Pat Robertson, apparently unaware that at the time he spoke five women were Grand Master chess players

On Running, Adventures While

An oversize brassiere might be considered a good investment if you are a runner who breast-feeds a very young baby and became pregnant while running.
from a U.S. government aerobics manual

On Running for President

Look, I'm trying to run for president! I can't sit here and debate free trade versus fair trade!
Pat Robertson in an interview during his run for the presidency

On Russian Invasions of Neighboring Countries, One Congressman's Views On

Look at it from the Russians' point of view—they only want a stable neighbor.

Representative Ron Dellums (D, Calif.) speaking on the Russian invasion of Afghanistan

On Sad Duties

I would be remorse in my duties if I didn't vote no.

Jasper Weese, Traverse City, Michigan, councilman during a City Commission meeting

On Saddam Hussein, Great Senatorial Foresight About

I have been sitting here and listening to you for an hour, and I am now aware that you are a strong and intelligent man and that you want peace. . . . I believe, Mr. President, that you can be a very influential force for peace in the Middle East.

Senator Howard Metzenbaum (D, Ohio) in a meeting with Iraqi president Saddam Hussein in 1990

On San Francisco, Pithy Royal Views Of

Aren't there any *male* supervisors? This is a nanny city.
Prince Philip of Great Britain upon meeting five San Francisco city officials—who were all women

On <u>Schindler's List</u>, Politician's View Of

I cringe when I realize that there were children all across this nation watching this program. They were exposed to the violence of multiple head wounds, vile language, full frontal nudity and irresponsible sexual activity. It simply should not have been allowed on public television.

Representative Tom Coburn (R, Okla.) after the broadcast premiere of Schindler's List *on NBC*

On Second Ladies, Totally Spontaneous Photo Ops With

She's going to be shoveling mud. Then she'll wipe the sweat from her brow, like this. Make sure you get that shot, all right?

Nathan Naylor, Vice President Al Gore's press spokesman, briefing network television crews right before Tipper Gore arrived on the scene in Honduras to "help" with the devastation of Hurricane Mitch

On Secret Anti-Arkansas Conspiracies

I think a lot of this is prejudice against our state. They wouldn't be doing this if we were from some other state.

Hillary Clinton complaining to the Arkansas Democrat-Gazette *that her husband was being investigated because of an anti-Arkansas bias*

On Secretaries of Defense, Problems of Figuring Out What a War Is

Reporter:

Are we at war with Yugoslavia?

Secretary of Defense William Cohen:

We're certainly engaged in hostilities. We're engaged in combat. Whether that measures up to, quote, a classic definition of war, I'm not qualified to say.

On Secretaries of State, Bad Role Models for Everyone Else

She is a woman after all. Rattling rockets and bombs—it is simply against nature.

Russian Communist Party leader Gennadi Zyuganov explaining that U.S. secretary of state Madeleine Albright was shaming women around the world through her frequent support of the use of military force

On Secretaries of State, Personal Role Models Of

One of my role models, Xena the Warrior Princess, comes from here.
Secretary of State Madeleine Albright during a trip to New Zealand

On Segues, Bad

Speaking of animals, he married his wife, Suzanne, when he was in college.

Utah governor Mike Leavitt introducing Senator Larry Craig with an extremely bad segue—for which he later apologized

On Self-Assessment, Odd

I would have made a good pope.
President Richard Nixon

On the Senate, Truth About

There are a lot of things we do that are irrelevant, but that's what the Senate is for.

Senator Alan Simpson (R, Wyo.) on the MacNeil/Lehrer NewsHour

On Senate Hearings, Great Moments In

Senator Helms:

Now, Mrs. Harriman, I know that you are involved in the Monnet Society. Monnet, of course, one of the spiritual founders of the European Community.

Mrs. Harriman:

Senator, I do not think I am involved in the Monnet Society. I never heard of it, frankly.

Senator Helms:

I believe the information submitted says that. Is that not correct?

Mrs. Harriman:

Oh, it is *Claude Monet,* Senator. It is the painter, the artist. His home is in France, it is called Giverny, where Claude Monet lived and painted. And I have given a contribution to help restore his home.

Senate Foreign Relations hearings on Pamela Harriman's nomination as Ambassador to France

On Senatorial Quips, Not So Cute

Q:

How can you live in Washington, D.C., with African-Americans?

Senator Conrad Burns (R, Mont.):

It's a hell of a challenge.

On Shampoo Theory, Ideological

I never use shampoo with milk or eggs. These are imperialist ideas. *Libyan leader Muammar el-Qaddafi quoted in the* Seattle Post-Intelligencer

On Shoes, Unusual

You want me to vote with the people back there with fine suits and alligator shoes snapping at their kneecaps?

Representative John Travis (D, Jackson) during a debate in the Louisiana state legislature

On Shutting Down the Famous Train Line, The Texas Eagle

Thank you for your letter regarding the protection of the Texas eagle. . . . I share your view that the urgent problem of species extinction and the conservation of biological diversity should be addressed. . . . I look forward to working with you for the future of our planet.

Vice President Al Gore responding to a letter from an elderly couple who were concerned that Amtrak was going to shut down its Texas Eagle line

On Simple Yet Complicated

Equal Employment Opportunity Commission (EEOC) chairman Gilbert Casellas:

The [Equal Opportunity] law's fairly clear, it's fairly simple.

Reporter John Stossel:

If you come to me applying for a job, and your arm's in a sling, can I ask you why your arm is in a sling?

EEOC chairman Casellas:

You can ask—you know what? I'm going to ask you to stop the tape . . . we're getting into a complicated area.

from a taped television interview (Stossel followed up by saying, "You run the EEOC and you don't even understand the rules?")

Big Money

Politicians unable to survive on their salaries often opt for outside income, helpfully provided by patriotic lobbyists, noble-minded business groups, and sharing, caring multimillionaires. We can only be pleased to learn that our politicians accept their honoraria for the most patriotic of reasons: to make America a better, more democratic place for all.

On $10,000 Speaking Fees, Purely Patriotic Reasons for Accepting

I accept honoraria. I do not like to do it. . . . We do have grandchildren to educate. . . . If it were not for their grandparents, one of these grandsons would not be graduating as a physics major this year. Another grandchild would not be entering as a freshman to college this year. It is important that this country graduate physics majors, majors in mathematics, chemistry, and various other disciplines in order to keep this country ahead in technology, science, and physics.

Senator Robert Byrd (D, W. Va.)

On Paris Junkets, Very, Very Vital

Reporter Lisa Myers:

[What was the purpose of your recent Paris junket?]

Representative Earl Hilliard (D, Ala.):

We may have, because of the things we did, averted World War Three. We don't know. And we will never know.

(Representative Hilliard, recently named the most traveled congressperson, spent well over a month abroad, as a member of the Agriculture and Small Business Committees)

On Singer Basketball Players, Amazing

I tell you, that Michael Jackson is unbelievable, isn't he? Three plays in twenty seconds!

Vice President Al Gore commenting on Michael Jordan's play during the 1998 NBA finals (Senator Orrin Hatch commented, "Anybody who calls Michael Jordan Michael Jackson is doing a lot worse than misspelling potato.")

On the Skin, Fascinating Facts from OSHA About

The skin is an important interface between man and the environment.

from an OSHA document on skin diseases

On Skin Diseases, Little-Known Facts About

Drinking is the cause of psoriasis.

Secretary of Health and Human Services Donna Shalala—intending to refer to cirrhosis, the liver disease, instead of the heartbreak of psoriasis, the skin disease

On Slavery, Political Justification Of

People who are bitter and hateful about slavery are obviously bitter and hateful against God and his word, because they reject what God says and embrace what mere humans say concerning slavery.

Alabama state senator Charles Davidson (R, Tuscaloosa County) explaining in a speech that the Bible justified slavery (quoting from Leviticus—"You may acquire male and female slaves from the pagan nations that are around you")

On Smoke Screens

I didn't like it and I didn't inhale it.

President Bill Clinton coyly explaining his marijuana usage on MTV

On Smoke Screen Defenses

I was trying to say that I actually tried. I was not trying to exonerate myself when I said I didn't inhale. . . . The important message is that these things are dangerous, that I wish I'd never done any of that, although I did such a little bit.

President Bill Clinton telling Barbara Walters about the MTV comment "I didn't inhale."

On Smoke Screens

I'm allergic to cigars so I don't smoke many anymore. . . . And I try not to do it in any way that sets a bad example. . . . I try never to do it where people see.

President Bill Clinton in a 1995 press conference—long before the famous incident with Monica and the cigar came to light

On Snappy Answers

The best example of all to me that our problems are both personal and cultural and political and social is the whole condition of the middle class economically.

President Bill Clinton at Georgetown University, July 6, 1995

On Snappy Electioneering

Obviously, I'd be proud to be in the home of the Bobcats. Bob Cat. Keep that in mind. We've never had a Bob in the White House. Don't you think it's time? Yeah. Right. We do have a cat in the White House. Socks. But we don't have a Bob in the White House.

Bob Dole campaigning at Grand Blanc High School in Michigan, home of the Bobcats

On Snappy Interviewing Questions You're Allowed to Ask a Communist Leader

Will Cuba be led into the next century by you? Which was your favorite American leader? Which was your favorite Soviet leader? What was the most amusing part of the Revolution?

list of questions entitled "Questions Castro Will Answer" included as part of Cuban leader Fidel Castro's book proposal for History Will Absolve Me: The Autobiography of Fidel Castro—*which also promised that "the author . . . will be available to promote [the book]"*

On Snowballing Mushrooms

[The issue is] a little snowball that rolled down the hill, that gathered moss, and when it got to the bottom, became a big mushroom.

Baltimore City Council member describing a particularly thorny issue

On Sore Losers, Not Very Conciliatory Words From

[The Wellington Labour Party is full of] loony left-wing socialists. . . . If you are a butch lesbian, you've got a better chance of being selected than someone who's straight.

Ian Gaskin, Labour Party Onslow electorate chairman, complaining about the party's Wellington local committee, after he wasn't nominated for a by-election

On Sore Losers, Wise Words From

Would she [Loretta Sanchez] have won with the name Larry Stafford? Play that mental game and you get an idea of the free ride a woman gets.

Representative Bob Dornan (R, Calif.) after losing the 1996 election to Loretta Sanchez

On Speaking a Little Too Soon

We may well see a woman as president in our lifetime. But it won't be Elizabeth Dole in the year 2000.

Elizabeth "Liddy" Dole in 1997

On Special Jobs for Monica Lewinsky at the U.S. Mission to the United Nations, Great Moments of Justification And

It's a fungible slot. You can trace a slot, but you can't say this person held that particular position because the position has evolved. It's such a nuance. What the senators were focused on—I mean, I gotta tell you, you're kind of getting into things that are really splitting hairs. People who held this job previously shouldn't regard themselves as the people who held the Monica slot. The job has evolved. All the allegations that people try to suggest, for example, that we created the job just for Monica, that doesn't hold up. Because regardless of Monica and prior to me ever knowing Monica Lewinsky was ever going to be anyone in the newspaper, I continued to have that need and I filled it.

Rebecca Cooper, chief of staff to then U.N. ambassador Bill Richardson, insisting that a special job was not created for Monica Lewinsky at the U.N.

On Specifications, Hard to Follow

I don't want any information. I just want the facts.
attributed to Calgary councilman John Kushner

On Speeches, Visionary

I can see Georgia leading the way. . . . I can see a country strong enough to defend itself. . . . I can see a country proud enough and competitive enough. . . . I can see a country that knows the difference between illegal immigration and legal immigration. . . . I can see a country with schools that are as good as our colleges. . . . I can see a country where the abortion rate and the divorce rate are headed down.

Lamar Alexander, presidential candidate

On Spelling, Congressional

Tudors Needed.

Jim Bacchus, Florida congressman, in a letter to other representatives "looking for volunteers to tutor underachieving high school students"

On Spelling, Vice Presidential

That's fine phonetically, but you're missing just a little bit.

Vice President Dan Quayle to William Figueroa, Trenton, New Jersey, sixth-grader, upon seeing the boy's (correct) spelling of the word pota-to, *which Quayle thought needed an* e *at the end*

On Spins, Dizzying

This is the first time my desire to put a spin on events has crossed the line from an honest discussion of my views to an exaggeration that turned out to be inaccurate.

political consultant Ed Rollins after he publicly stated, then retracted, that the New Jersey Republicans—for whom he was working—had paid half a million dollars to black ministers and Democratic workers to keep Democratic voter turnout low

On Spins, Not So Good

They made an animal-type grunting sound when the National Guard was mentioned. There were some good-natured grunts. Let me admit theoretically that some people hissed.

David Beckwith, press secretary to Vice President Dan Quayle, commenting on rumors that West Point cadets hissed at Quayle

On Splitting Hairs, Definitional

The word *shall* in the statute requiring prosecution doesn't really mean "shall"; it means "may or may not."

U.S. Attorney Stanley Harris on why the Justice Department was not charging former head of the Environmental Protection Agency Anne Burford with contempt of Congress

On Splitting Hairs, Gifted

I didn't accept it. I received it.

Richard Allen, national security adviser to President Reagan, explaining the $1,000 in cash and two watches he was given by two Japanese journalists after he helped arrange a private interview for them with First Lady Nancy Reagan

On Splitting Hairs, Hair-Raising

The term *forced busing* is a misnomer [because children] don't have to ride a bus, but only to arrive on time at their assigned schools.

Clinton Justice Department civil-rights appointee Bill Lann Lee

On Splitting Hairs, Taxing

I haven't committed a crime. What I did was fail to comply with the law.

David Dinkins, New York City mayor, answering accusations that he failed to pay his taxes

On Spontaneous, Unstudied Answers to the Question "Do You Know the Price of Milk?"

A dollar eighty-nine here, and two dollars and sixty-nine in New Jersey. It's one ninety-nine in New Hampshire.

multimillionaire presidential candidate Steve Forbes showing his middle-class knowledge

On State Agencies, Chatty

Texas Natural Resource Conversation Commission

envelopes from the Texas state conservation agency

On State Department Bureaucrats, In-the-Know

Senator Joe Biden:

Can you tell me who is the prime minister of South Africa?

William Clark (nominated to be deputy secretary of state):

No, sir, I cannot.

Biden:

Can you tell me who the president of Zimbabwe is?

Clark:

It would be a guess.

Biden:

What are the countries in Europe, in NATO, that are most reluctant to go along with theater nuclear-force modernization?

Clark:

I am not in a position . . . to categorize them from the standpoint of acceptance on one hand and resistance on the other.

William Clark, a California judge and rancher, nominated for deputy secretary of state, during his confirmation hearing before the Senate Foreign Relations Committee—after which he was immediately confirmed. Two years later, he became national security adviser.

On the State of Alabama, Totally, Completely, Absolutely Unprejudiced

I've never seen any anti-Semitism in Alabama. I don't think anti-Semitism exists in the state of Alabama.

Republican governor Fob James of Alabama during a trip to Israel

On the Status Quo

Only one thing would be worse than the status quo. And that would be for the status quo to become the norm.

Elizabeth Dole in a 1999 campaign speech

On the Status Quo, Unchangeability Of

If we don't make some changes, the status quo will remain the same.
member of President Bill Clinton's staff

On Martha Stewart, What Not to Say To

Martha, just what is it that you do?
Colorado governor Roy Romer being introduced to Martha Stewart at a White House dinner

On Stiff Upper Lips, Snarling

I cannot think of anybody else I would sooner not appoint to this post. She is a lady short on looks, absolutely deprived of any dress sense, has a figure like a Jurassic monster, is very greedy when it comes to loot, and wants to upstage everyone else.
Sir Nicholas Fairbairn, British politician, on the appointment of Sarah Ferguson, the Duchess of York, as a U.N. envoy

The Worst Political Jokes

Politicians are eager to prove they're just one of the guys (or gals, as the case may be). And how better to prove this than with a fun little knee-slapping, ice-breaking attempt at humor? (Note: *Attempt* is the key word here.)

It's the old toastmaster trick—soften up the crowd with a laugh, then move on to more serious matters. And, in truth, many politicians are masters of the art of the well-timed joke. But there are others . . .

On Jokes, Bad Taste In

Do you know why Chelsea Clinton is so ugly? Because Janet Reno is her father!

Senator John McCain (R, Ariz.) at a Republican fund-raiser

On Jokes about Africa, Dubious

When those countries have a man to lunch, they really have him to lunch.

Ronald Reagan, then Republican candidate for governor of California, talking about emerging African nations

On Political Wives, Not That Great Jokes About

It [a champion country ham] reminds me of my wife. It's expensive, but it's mighty good.

Governor John Y. Brown Jr. (R, Ky.) cutely comparing the costly ham he had just gotten at an auction with his wife, former Miss America Phyllis George Brown

---

On Stock Ownership, Politicians And

I don't see any kind of conflict of interest for anybody, unless they have a controlling interest—fifty-one percent of a bank or something.

Texas state senator Chet Brooks on why his bank stocks and bank loans didn't create a conflict of interest on his voting on bank legislation

On Stool Analogies in Speeches, Confusing

What we need to do in this campaign is unleash a people power that is second to none and make people think and realize that there is help. So the church becomes an important leg of this stool and without it the stool is going to collapse. I want a strong leg . . . and as we make that stool, it's got to stand up on its legs. And it's got to be able to take the seat of that stool and do what it should be, and that is turn people on to how right it can be in the state of California.

Senator Dianne Feinstein (D, Calif.) running for governor of California, in a speech in Oakland

On Straight Answers

Reporter:

Will the consumer price index be revised?

Health and Human Resources Secretary Richard Schweiker:

Let me be explicit. This administration may be looking at across-the-board revision, or nonrevision, of the index.

On Student Loans, Why You Don't Need As Long As Parents Foot the Skiing Bills

I can't understand all the fuss about student grants. Carol managed to save out of hers. Of course, we paid for her skiing holidays.

Margaret Thatcher, prime minister of England, talking about how easy it is to save for college

On Students, Ones Who Have Been Kept Back Again and Again

There is a group of students that have been going to school in the state of Arkansas since the turn of the century.

Representative Pinky Wilkerson (D, Grambling) during a debate in the Louisiana state legislature

On Success, Retreating

The people of Texas want us to secede.
Governor William Clements, meaning "succeed"

On the Suez Canal, What to Say When You First See It

This is beautiful. I've always wanted to see the Persian Gulf.
Senator William Scott (R, Va.) to his host, Egyptian president Anwar Sadat, while looking at the Suez Canal

On Superclever Tips on How to Get Elected

From an article offering twenty-five ways for a candidate to win, in a July 1997 Campaigns & Elections: The Magazine for Political Professionals:

Tip #2: Figure out on your own what you stand for.

On Supervisory Biologists in Government, Mentally Challenged

Minorities, women, and the mentally challenged are strongly encouraged to apply.

job announcement put out by the United States Department of the Interior, National Biological Survey

On Supporting Your Candidate, Not-So-Great Reasons For

I'm staying with [Dole] because I believe that he doesn't believe all the crap his handlers have been having him say.

Ohio governor George Voinovich

On Surprises, Unsurprising

This is a delightful surprise to the extent that it is a surprise, and it is only a surprise to the extent that we anticipated.

Secretary of State James Baker

On Surrealism, Presidential

I've been criticized for doing more than one thing at once. . . . Would it be nice if you could pay your bills and not earn any money to them? I don't understand this whole—you can't do one thing at once. But anyway, that's what they say.

President Bill Clinton at an appearance at a Cleveland shopping mall

On Surrealism, Watergate-Style

That is, because of, because of our, that is, we are attempting, the position is to withhold information and to cover up—this is totally true—you could say it is totally untrue.

President Richard Nixon from 1973 White House transcripts, discussing whether or not to hide evidence concerning the Watergate break-in

On Syntax, Presidential

I'm working on funding it just as close to what I recommended during the campaign, about putting people first.

President Bill Clinton

On Syntax, Presidential

We didn't give a timetable, but we've encouraged in every way these and more. But I'm just asking that people look at them. I have not seen them—maybe it's my fault—on account of whatever media of these steps put together as a package. Haven't seen one. So I'd like to suggest to the congress that are debating this to take a hard look at this and see whether it's progress, whether it adds up to anything or, as some of our critics would say, it's pure, you know, boilerplate.

former president George Bush

On Take My Assemblyman, Please!

The first thing she [newly installed Speaker Doris Allen] ought to do is her hair.

California state assemblyman Bill Morrow (R, Oceanside) when asked what he thought the new Speaker of the House, Doris Allen, ought to do

On Take My House Speaker, Please!

I cook occasionally just to see how easy women's work is.

House Speaker Thomas P. O'Neill

On Take My Representative, Please!

I feel we made one serious mistake when we gave the vote to women.
Representative John Monks

On Take My State Senator, Please!

Do you know why God created woman? Because sheep can't type.
Texas state senator Kenneth Armbrister

On Take My Third-Party Organizer, Please!

They are trying to prove their manhood.
Ross Perot during his presidential campaign, about women reporters who ask tough questions

On Taking a Stand, Great Political Moments, Part 1

Let me suggest that I support the exceptions for rape, incest, life of the mother, and I would do pretty much as Bill, as Pat Buchanan indicates in this case. I want to make that clear; I thought we had just a short answer. But I wanted to underscore my strong pro-life record for people who have that view, and again, I think we can have different views and still be good Republicans.

Senator Bob Dole in 1996, elucidating his strong pro-anti-in-the-middle attitude on abortion

On Taking a Stand, Great Political Moments, Part 2

The federal government should stay entirely out of it [the abortion issue] because I believe it's wrong and that states may restrict it. I would characterize those views as pro-life. But I think we need to move on.

Lamar Alexander, presidential candidate

On Taking Drugs, Traitorous

It is a disloyal, treasonous act to use illegal substances in this country, and let us get that clear.

Representative Bob Dornan (R, Calif.)

On Talk, Educational

We've given priorities within the learning-materials-development plan to the development of curriculum materials in these particular areas. The thrust of our multiculturalism policy is inputted to all our curriculum-guideline committees and into our evaluation and research committees.

Tom Wells, education minister in the Ontario provincial parliament

On Talking, What Not to Do When

Don't just sort of talk in words.

Tom Wells, education minister in the Ontario provincial parliament

On Tax Breaks for Corporations, One Congressman's Principled Defense

The corporate-welfare thing is overplayed. It's difficult to define. Someone can be the life of the party or a drunk, depending on the perspective.

Representative Ralph Regula (R, Ohio)

On Tax Returns, Filing Instructions for Criminals

Illegal income, such as stolen or embezzled money, must be included in your gross income.

helpful information posted on the official Internal Revenue Service Web site

On Taxes, Excited

The public is fed up with exuberant taxes.

New Jersey state senator Anthony Imperiale

On Teaching, Clear Moments In

You can now get a certificate to teach German by sitting through enough classes, but if you speak German, you can't teach German if you don't have a certificate. So you can have a German teacher who can't speak German, but though they have the certificate so they can teach, even though they can't teach. . . . If you can speak it, you can't teach it, even if you could teach it. Are you with me so far?

House Speaker Newt Gingrich

On Technology, the Final Word On

High tech is potent, precise, and in the end, unbeatable. The truth is, it reminds a lot of people of the way I pitch horseshoes. Would you believe some of the people? Would you believe our dog? Look, I want to give the high-five symbol to high tech.

President George Bush

On Telling It All

The [deleted] is a key element of the Worldwide Military Command and Control System (WWMCCS) warning network. . . . [Deleted] currently consists of [deleted] satellite; two [deleted] satellites; an [deleted] for [deleted] from the [deleted] satellite; a [deleted] for [deleted] and the [deleted] satellites; and a [deleted] which provides [deleted] for the [deleted]. . . . Using these data, [deleted] can be inferred.

a portion of an arms control impact statement submitted to Congress by the Pentagon

On Testimonials, Not-So-Stirring

The bottom line is there have been a lot of nuts elected to the United States Senate.

Senator Charles Grassley (R, Iowa) on why Republicans should support Oliver North for his Senate run in 1994

On Testimony, Dancing

I hope there would be no inconsistency. . . . that they would all jive correctly.

Clinton secretary Betty Currie answering questions about differences in her testimony on different days

On Thank-Yous, Damp

I cannot tell you how grateful I am—I am filled with humidity.
Gib Lewis, Speaker of the Texas House

On Thanks for Clearing That Up

I don't know what these other guys are running for. I want to be president of the United States. I don't want an ad agency, never wanted an ad agency. I don't run a magazine.

Senator Bob Dole (R, Kans.)

On That Old-Time Religion Thing

I think in politics there are certain moral values. I'm one who—we believe strongly in separation of church and state, but then you get into some questions there are some moral overtones. Murder, that kind of thing, and I feel a little, I will say uncomfortable with the elevation of the religious thing.

President George Bush on Meet the Press, *talking about the relationship between church and state*

On That Wacky Nixon White House, Instructions From

Please burn before reading.

1972 White House memo on illegal campaign tactics being planned against Democratic candidate George McGovern

On There's a Good Reason Here

The president was somewhat mystified as to why there was no mention of him in the 3 October 1995 article in the *Arkansas Democrat Gazette* entitled "Sex Can Wait plan gets $200,000 grant."

memo from Harold Ickes, Clinton adviser, to Secretary of Health and Human Services Donna Shalala

---

The Most Gripping Political Rhetoric

"Friends, Romans, countrymen, lend me your, um . . . uhhh . . . ehh . . . ers!"

This could well be a rallying cry for many politicians. Hoping for rhetorical brilliance (or even rhetorical not-so-badness), they ruefully discover that their tongues are not silver, but lead. Words don't fall trippingly off the tongue. Instead, the tongue trips.

These examples of oration are breathtaking indeed . . . but the breath that is taken is the speaker's —who is caught in a vicious circle of *um*s, *er*s, *uh*s, and *ah*s. Nevertheless, the listener is mesmerized . . . although not *quite* in the way the would-be rhetorician intended. Instead, the listener is laying down mental bets, wondering if the politician will ever actually make it to the end of a complete sentence.

On Clear Answers

I am not. I'm sorry I should. You want me to re-repeat that, the, the question is that, uh, I'm sorry that we don't have a public address for the—the question is do I agree with Senator Dirksen's and Senator—and—and Congressman Ford's position—uh—that—uh, Vice President Humphrey's position has only partisan motivation? Tha—tha—that they are new policies that have only partisan motivation—eh—uh—part—eh—partisan—sorry—uh—would you—why don't you read it loud enough so they can all hear?

President Richard Nixon

On Gab, the Gift Of

Well, I think that's a—it's had some difficult times but I think we have—we, I think, have been able to make some very good progress and it's—I would say that it's—it's—it's delightful that we're able to—to share the time and the relationship that we—that we do share.

Senator Ted Kennedy during a November 4, 1979, on-air interview with Roger Mudd, trying to answer the question "What is the present state of your marriage?"

239

On Things Affirmative-Action Directors Shouldn't Call Dwarves

Midget.

Houston affirmative action director Lenoria Walker, referring to city councilman Joe Roach, who is a dwarf

On Things Not to Say on Live TV after Losing an Election

Well, shit!

Nashville councilman Ludye Wallace expressing his sentiments on television after losing a 1995 election

On Things We'd Rather Not Know

Hattie, I'm horny.

former Arizona governor Bruce Babbitt to his wife during his Democratic presidential campaign. He didn't realize the microphone was on.

On Things We've Never Said

Sometimes I would rather have a gun than a banana.

Representative Steve Gunn (Is, Montgomery) during a debate in the Louisiana state legislature

On Things We've Never Thought About

Life is very important to Americans.
Senator Bob Dole (R, Kans.) when asked if American lives were more important than foreign lives

On Things We've Never Thought About Wichita Falls

If we were twenty-five or thirty miles north of here, we would be the third-biggest city in Oklahoma.
Ronald J. Mertens, head of the Wichita Falls Board of Commerce

On Those Lazy Stay-at-Home Moms, Christopher Dodd's Take On

[Stay-at-home mothers have chosen not to work, but to stay at home because they] want to go play golf or go to the club and play cards.
Senator Chris Dodd (D, Conn.)

On Those Wimpy Women, One Politician's View

The idea that you can defend this nation within the Constitution, under the law, and tell the truth is still considered a sort of childish, feminine position.
Vice President Walter Mondale

On Thoughts That Shouldn't Be Thunk

When I got to thinking, the way we get thoroughbred horses and thoroughbred dogs is through inbreeding. Maybe we would get a super-sharp kid.

Carl Gunter, Louisiana House of Representatives, on why he opposes abortion for incest victims

On Tie Analogies, Great Moments In

I could tell you that I am not on this television show, making statements in a solid blue tie. Now I am on the television show. I'm making statements. But there are some . . . there are some polka dots on the tie.

Senator John Ashcroft (R, Mo.) elucidating political truth-telling practices

On Titles, Odd

The Village, the Village, the Earth, the Earth and the Suicide of the Astronaut

title of Libyan leader Muammar el-Qaddafi's book of short stories

On Tobacco, Why It's No Worse Than Many Other Things

We know it's not good for kids. But a lot of other things aren't good. Drinking's not good. Some would say milk's not good.

Senator Bob Dole during the 1996 presidential campaign

On Tolerance, Intolerant

I will not tolerate intolerance.
Senator Bob Dole on Pat Buchanan, his 1996 rival for the Republican presidential nomination

On Torture, Reassuring Facts About

I do not deny that torture continues to be used in this country, but there are strict orders to the army not to use torture.
Ernesto Geisel, president of Brazil

On Trees

A tree's a tree. How many more do you need to look at?
Ronald Reagan

On Trees, Further Thoughts On

When you see one redwood, you've seen them all.
Ronald Reagan

On Trees, Second Thoughts About

I don't believe a tree is a tree and if you've seen one, you've seen them all.
Ronald Reagan

On Tricky Technical Points, Bill Clinton's Mastery Of

They've managed to keep their unemployment low although their overall unemployment is high.

President Bill Clinton discussing taxes and employment

On Trust in the People, Presidential

We could give [the surplus] all back to you and hope you spend it right.

President Bill Clinton telling the people of Buffalo, New York, why it is better to have bureaucrats spend money than to have taxpayers spend it

On Truth

There are two kinds of truth. There are real truths and there are made-up truths.

Marion Barry, mayor of Washington, D.C., on his arrest for drug use

On the Truth, Sort Of

That is true—but not absolutely true.

Montreal mayor Jean Drapeau

On Truth in Government

I've had just about all of this good government stuff I can stand.
state senator Charles Jones (D, Monroe) during a debate in the Louisiana legislature

On Truth in Politics, Great Moments

This is the most important bill of the session. . . . I have not read the bill.
Representative Sherman Copelin (D, New Orleans) discussing a bill in the Louisiana legislature

On Truths, Political

I'm running for president of the United States because I believe that—with strong leadership—America's days will always lie ahead of us. Just as they lie ahead of us now.
Bob Dole campaigning during the 1996 presidential race

On Trying to Please Everyone, Bill Clinton And

I guess I would have voted with the majority if it was a close vote. But I agree with the arguments the minority made.
President Bill Clinton on the 1991 Gulf War resolution

On Turns of Phrase, Exciting

[I support] erection to resurrection coverage.

Oregon Democratic Senate candidate Tom Brugere explaining his support for comprehensive health care (He later changed his statement to "cradle-to-grave" coverage.)

On the Twentieth Century, Great Observations About

[The Holocaust] was an obscene period in our nation's history . . . this century's history. . . . We all lived in this century. I didn't live in this century.

Dan Quayle, then Indiana senator and Republican vice-presidential candidate, during a news conference in which he was asked his opinion about the Holocaust

On Twenty-Twenty Hindsight

You know, I've always wondered about the taping equipment. But I'm damn glad we have it.

President Richard Nixon to White House aide H. R. Haldeman

On Unanimity, Unusual

Our cabinet is always unanimous—except when we disagree.
Bill Bennett, premier of British Columbia, Canada, attempting to clearly state his cabinet's views on nuclear power plants

On the United States, Odd Goals Of

[The United States] will work toward the elimination of human rights.
Vice President Dan Quayle in a pledge to El Salvador

On the United States, Where Found

We have a firm commitment to NATO, we are a part of NATO. We have a firm commitment to Europe. We *are* a part of Europe.

Vice President Dan Quayle

On U.S. Forests, Why the Trees Look Kind of Droopy Recently

Only unqualified applicants may apply.

Only applicants who do not meet standards will be considered.

two separate position announcements for the U.S. Forest Service

On the U.S. Military, Proud Boasts About

I've lived under situations where every decent man declared war first and I've lived under situations where you don't declare war. We've been flexible enough to kill people without declaring war.

Lewis B. Hershey, lieutenant general and director of the Selective Service System

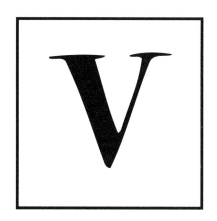

On Veggies, Meaty

Pasty-maker:
These are vegetarian pasties.
Lady Margaret Thatcher:
Lovely. And have you put much meat in them?

On Verbosity

Verbosity leads to unclear, inarticulate things.
Vice President Dan Quayle

On Verbs, New

I've tasked Bill. I've said, "Bill, work the problem."
President George Bush about drug czar William Bennett's job

On Verbs, New Political

We need to stiffify these penalties.
Representative John Travis (D, Jackson) during a Louisiana legislature debate about killing police dogs

On Vice-Presidential/Presidential Relations, a Little Too Close

For seven and a half years I've worked alongside President Reagan. We've had triumphs. Made some mistakes. We've had some sex . . . uh, setbacks.
President George Bush (then campaigning)

On Vice Presidents, a Little over the Top

They use their color-blind the way duck hunters use their duck blind! They hide behind the phrase and just hope that we, like the ducks, won't be able to see through it. We see through your color-blind! Amazing grace also saved me! Was color-blind but now I see! The Gospel of Luke tells us of Jesus' reaction to people who willfully refused to see the evidence before their eyes . . . ye hypocrites!

Vice President Al Gore

On Virtuality

In a sense, virtuality at the mental level is something I think you'd find in most leadership over historical periods.

Speaker of the House Newt Gingrich, from his "From Virtuality and Reality"

On Visits, Insightful Comments On

I haven't been to Michigan since the last time I was there.

attributed to Vice President Dan Quayle

On Voter Payoffs

That's just part of small-town politics. I've probably given out thousands of dollars over the past five years. A person is not going to vote for you for that reason.

South Carolina state representative Grady Brown, who outspent his opponent by over four times—and won

On Voting Problems, Arkansas-Style

No person shall be permitted, under any pretext whatever, to come nearer than fifty feet of any door or window of any polling room, from the opening of polls until the completion of the count and the certification of counted returns.

Arkansas law

The Best Bald-Faced Flip-Flops

The average person (which is to say, the nonpolitician) when caught in a 180-degree change of opinion tends to hem and haw, attempt explanation of the dramatic switch, and make frantic efforts of justification.

Not so the politician. Why draw attention to the fact that merely two days ago he said the reverse of what he is saying today (both times with heartfelt conviction, of course)? Why not instead shift directions and hope no one happens to notice?

This happy political ability to become a human flapjack—to cut loose from the past and focus only on the here and now in a sort of nonpartisan Zen manner—has resulted in some of the most fascinating examples of flip-flops . . . and sometimes flip-flop-flips.

On No Comment

I have no comment at all on that entire zone. And we'll cheerfully repeat that phrase as often as you all want to ask the question.

Newt Gingrich, then Speaker of the House, on February 11, 1998, commenting—or not commenting—on the Monica Lewinsky affair

I will never again, as long as I am Speaker, make a speech *without* commenting on this topic.

Newt Gingrich on April 27, 1998

I won't pay any attention to it.

Newt Gingrich on July 20, 1998

On Timing Is Everything

[Due to pollution, cars pose] a mortal threat to the security of every nation.

Senator Al Gore in his 1992 book, Earth in the Balance

Here in Motor City, we recognize that cars have done more than fuel our commerce. Cars have freed the American spirit and given us the chance to chase our dreams.

Vice President Al Gore—while gearing up for his 2000 presidential run—in a 1999 speech to the Economic Club of Detroit

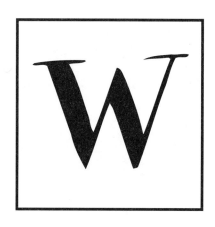

On Waffling

I'm not indecisive. Am I indecisive?
Jim Scheibel, mayor of St. Paul, Minnesota

On Wages, Parsley-Sprigged

I support a plan to garnish their wages.
President Bill Clinton in a 1998 speech about forcing delinquent fathers to pay child support

On Washington, D.C., Crime, Fascinating Facts About

If crime went down one hundred percent, it would still be fifty times higher than it should be.

Councilman John Bowman commenting on the high crime rate in Washington, D.C.

On Washington, D.C., Proud Boasts About

Outside of the killings, [Washington] has one of the lowest crime rates in the country.

Washington, D.C., mayor Marion Barry

On Washington Insiders, Washington Insider View Of

They've been in Washington too long. They talk Washington. They think Washington.

frequent presidential candidate, former governor of Tennessee, and former secretary of education under George Bush, Lamar Alexander, explaining that his opponents are all Washington "insiders" —an assertion about which Bob Dole once said, "Lamar's out there every day claiming he's an outsider. I remember meeting him when I came to Washington."

On Washingtonians, Toxic
The contagious people of Washington have stood firm against diversity during this long period of increment weather.
Marion Barry, mayor of Washington, D.C.

On Watergate, Freudian Slips And
This is a discredited president . . . precedent.
President Richard Nixon

On We Can Arrange That
If somebody's gonna stab me in the back, I wanna be there.
attributed to Toronto municipal politician Allan Lambert during a city council meeting

On What about Lincoln, Washington, Etc.
James Bond is a man of honor, a symbol of real value to the free world.
President Ronald Reagan

On What Not to Call People You're Negotiating With

. . . drunks and lickspittles.

characterization of Pacific negotiating partners found in a top-secret Australian diplomatic document accidentally left lying on a desk

On What Not to Call Your Opponents

Sambos.

the Reverend James Thomas, an African-American Galveston city councilman, referring to his opponents, also African-Americans

On What Not to Say about Your Co-Workers

I admit [Mines Minister Judy Ercola] has a nice body, but it's too bad it's connected to her mouth.

Gordon Taylor, member of Canadian Parliament

On What Not to Say to an African-American Audience

Sure, I look like a white man. But my heart is as black as anyone's here.

George Wallace, Alabama governor and then presidential candidate, during a campaign speech to a largely black audience

On What Not to Say to an Amputee During a Political Debate

Your walk says so much more than your talk.

Guy Millner, Republican senatorial candidate, during a debate with his opponent, Democrat Max Cleland—who is a triple amputee due to grenade injuries he got in Vietnam

On What Not to Say to a Female Reporter

Are you hot to trot this week?

Virginia state senator Hunter B. Andrews to a female reporter

On What Not to Say to a Restaurant Manager

Sir, I have been fingering your waitress for a long time, but she just does not want to come.

Joseph "Erap" Estrada, president of the Philippines, complaining to a restaurant manager when a waitress ignored his gestures and failed to come over to the table

On What Not to Say to Testifying Feminists

These are the prettiest witnesses we have had in a long time. I imagine you all are married. If not, you could be if you wanted to be.

Senator Strom Thurmond, addressing a group of women's leaders who were testifying before a Senate hearing

On What Not to Say to a Testifying Woman

It's only because you're so cute that I'm letting you get away with this.
Representative Joe Barton (R, Tex.) after the president of the Association for Commuter Transportation, Dee Angell, took too much time testifying before his committee

On What Not to Say to Voters in Wheelchairs

And now, will y'all stand and be recognized?
Gib Lewis, Texas Speaker of the House, on Disability Day, to a group of people in wheelchairs watching the House session

On What to Call the Nicaraguan Contras

Freeder fightoms.
Senator Bob Dole attempting to praise the Nicaraguans during an NBC interview—but getting a little tongue-tied

On What to Say If You're Handed a Romanian Flag

Thanks for the poncho.
President Bill Clinton when given the Romanian flag during a 1997 visit to Romania. In fairness, the flag had a hole in the middle—where the communist emblem used to be—as postrevolution, people want to eradicate symbols of Communism

On What to Say to People in Soup Kitchens

Do you come here often?

Senator Ted Kennedy (D, Mass.) politely chatting with a soup-kitchen patron

On What to Say to Samoans

You all look like happy campers to me. Happy campers you are, happy campers you have been, and as far as I am concerned, happy campers you will always be.

Vice President Dan Quayle addressing a group of Samoans during a Pacific trip

On What You Think of When You've Been Shot Down

I was shot down, and I was floating around in my little yellow raft, setting a record for paddling. I thought of my family, my mom and my dad, and the strength I got from them. I thought of my faith, the separation of church and state.

President George Bush

On White House Press Releases, Urgent News In

Details of the First Lady Hillary Rodham Clinton's Attire. . . . Visit to Piazza Navona: A two-piece fuschia Noviello Bloom suit of a linen blend. The buttons close the front of the jacket creating a lovely U-shape opening at the neck. Bone shoes and a matching purse finish the suit. The Vatican: As a sign of respect for the tradition of the Vatican, a black Dana Buchman long-sleeved silk dress was chosen for Mrs. Clinton's audience with the pope. The dress wraps and ties at the waist. In accordance with the traditional requirements, a mantilla will be worn to cover Mrs. Clinton's head. All other accessories are pearl with gold accents.

White House press release issued during a presidential trip to Europe

On Who Needs Food When You've Got a Computer

I'm just tossing this out . . . but maybe we need a tax credit for the poorest Americans to buy a laptop.

former House Speaker Newt Gingrich

On Why Boll-Weevil-Eradication Legislation Should Be Discussed During an Anticrime Session

Well, it involves killing and capital punishment.
Louisiana state representative Noble Ellington (D, Winnsboro) trying to explain why his boll-weevil-eradication bill fit into an anticrime session

On Why Federal Security Guards Were Wearing Rubber Gloves When They Greeted Gay and Lesbian Politicians

It was an error in judgment, apparently.
White House press secretary Mike McCurry trying to explain why federal security guards wore rubber gloves at a White House meeting of gay and lesbian politicians—that President Clinton decided not to attend

On Why It's Okay for Senators to Appear in a Television Commercial for a Military Contractor

I'm the former chairman of the Ethics Committee. I know what's ethical and what isn't, and there is nothing unethical about this.
Senator Ted Stevens (R, Alaska)

On Why Members of Congress Deserve a Raise (from the Over $133,600 They Earn)

I will tell you something. Members of this House have families. They have two homes, in most cases. Some members are living in their offices because they cannot afford a second residence. . . . I am not making excuses or apologizing. It is difficult to raise a family and serve in congress under these conditions. . . . [My] wife and my children sacrifice enough.

Congressman Tom DeLay (R, Tex.) calling for an "inflation adjustment"—or, as it's more commonly called by noncongressmen, a "raise"—and explaining that he just couldn't make ends meet on just $133,600 in salary (not including any speech fees or honoraria that he may have received)

On Why Not?

What we have is two important values in conflict: freedom of speech and our desire for healthy campaigns and a healthy democracy. You can't have both.

Representative Dick Gephardt (D, Mo.) on campaign finance reform

On Why We Don't Have Judge Mickey

Mickey Mouse is not and has not been a resident of Comal County for six months as required by law.

part of Comal County, Texas, election officials' petition to deny the win to Mickey Mouse, who was the write-in candidate against a judge running unopposed

On Why You Should Be Sure Your Microphone Is Off, Part 1

I have no scruples. What is good, we take advantage of. What is bad, we hide.

Brazilian finance minister Rubens Ricupero during a break in a television-interview taping, speaking off-the-cuff about economic indicators to the interviewer—and not aware that the satellite feed was still running . . . and viewers all over the country could hear him

On Why You Should Be Sure Your Microphone Is Off, Part 2

Listen, just between us, it might seem presumptuous, but the government needs me a lot more than I need it. You know, I never say this, but there are innumerable people who write me to say they are only voting for him [President Itamar Franco] because of me. I'm his biggest vote-getter.

Ricupero further expounding during the taping break—and still unaware that the feed was broadcasting him live (He resigned two days later.)

On Why You Should Be Sure . . .

I was a victim of an electronic breakdown!
Brazilian finance minister Rubens Ricupero's novel defense

On Winning the Christian Vote, What Not to Say

And the cross, I love that, too. We wear crosses around our necks—
you know, it's like Lenny Bruce said: "Why don't we wear the f-ing elec-
tric chairs around our neck?"
Geoffrey Feiger, at the time Dr. Jack Kevorkian's lawyer, making one of
his blunt comments in an interview that later came back to haunt him
when he was running for governor of Michigan

On Winning the Jewish Vote, What Not to Say

[The group of Orthodox rabbis are] closer to Nazis than they think.
Geoffrey Feiger, then Democratic candidate in the Michigan guberna-
torial race

On Winning the Women's Vote, What Not to Say

Linda, because she is a lady, is afraid of math.
George Brown, Democratic candidate for California's Assembly, after
hearing that his Republican opponent, Linda Wilde, said she believed the
Department of Education should be eliminated

On Wisdom, Presidential

Let me give you a little serious political advice. One single word. Puppies. Worth the points.

President George Bush

On with Friends Like This . . .

Surprised he didn't auction off a place in his own bedroom. He'd probably sleep on the floor if somebody gave him a million.

former political adviser Bill Morris on his former client Bill Clinton

On Wives, Distracting

She is my whole heart, that one. And it only adds to her charm that she is of Cuban distraction.

Hugh Rodham—Hillary Clinton's brother, who was then trying to nab Florida's Democratic nomination for the Senate—about his wife

On Wives, Unenlightened

If you get married, sex is part of the contract.

Texas state representative Patricia Hill (Dallas) explaining why she voted against a bill making rape by a husband a crime

On Women

It is true that women who marry do give up some rights, but they gain the benefit of guaranteed support.

Washington state senator George Clarke, explaining why he was against a law citing rape by a husband as a crime

On Women

Jeremiah plainly tells us that when the people of a nation are willing to accept the leadership of a woman, it is a sure sign of God's curse.

the Reverend Everett Sileven, Nebraska gubernatorial candidate—who was defeated

On Women, Soo Naive

[Women are] not going to understand throw weights or what is happening in Afghanistan or what is happening in human rights.

Donald Regan, President Reagan's chief of staff, explaining why he thought women didn't have much of a role to play in politics

On Women, Wimpy

[Women are] less equipped psychologically to "stay the course" in the brawling arenas of business, commerce, industry, and the professions.

Pat Buchanan, conservative columnist and frequent candidate for the Republican presidential nomination

On Women, As Opposed to People, Pat Buchanan's View On

I don't think we should have to have them wandering the streets frightening women and people.

presidential candidate Patrick Buchanan on why homeless people should be locked up

On Women in Office

You're talking about a housewife running for mayor who, to my way of thinking, cannot devote as much time as I have to the office. A real fine lady is devoted to her husband and children and the activities of the home.

Mayor Joe Dienhart

On Women in Politics, Enlightened Views On

Right now, the issues are being ignored because Nebraska is running this state prom-queen contest and calling it a governor's race.

Nebraska state senator John DeCamp commenting on Nebraska's gubernatorial race—which was between two women candidates

On Women in the Military

Part of the great success was the fact that we have an all-volunteer army, and part of the all—the military. And part of the rationale is people will have more say in what they want to do. So another—I want to be part of this. I can respect that and understand it.

President George Bush speaking about women in the military

On Women's Sports, Avid Fans Of

We never had total equality in women's athletics, and I don't know that we ever will have. . . . There is no women's wrestling. I guess there's women's mud wrestling.

Henry Bellmon, governor of Oklahoma

On Working-Class Champions, Great Moments For

Representative David Bonior (D, Mich.):

"primary residence": $39,000 condo in "lower-middle-class area" of Michigan

"D.C. (secondary) residence": $318,000 home (in a community that excludes those who have not "achieved recognized status in a professional field")

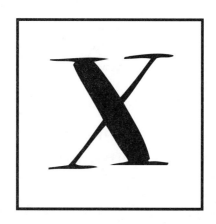

On X-Rated Moments in the Georgia State Assembly

Mr. Speaker, will you please turn me on?

Georgia state representative Anne Mueller, complaining to the Georgia Speaker, Tom Murphy, that her microphone was turned off (Speaker Murphy responded: "Thirty years ago, I would have tried.")

On X-Rated Moments in Political Debates

Walter Mondale (Democratic candidate):

George Bush doesn't have the manhood to apologize.

George Bush (Republican candidate):

Well, on the manhood thing, I'll put mine up against his anytime.

On X-Rated Moments in Provincial Legislature

Mr. Speaker! Mr. Speaker! Won't you please bang that thing of yours on the table!

Agnes Kripps, Canadian Socred, to the Speaker of the British Columbia legislature, during a heated discussion on sexual terminology

On Your Tax Dollars at Work, Great Moments in Specifying Proper Government Ashtrays for Cigarettes, Which You Can't Smoke in Government Buildings:

Type I, square, 4½ inch (114.3 mm) ashtray (Ash Receivers, Tobacco [desk type]) must include:

A minimum of four cigarette rests, spaced equidistant around the periphery and aimed at the center of the receiver, molded into the top. The cigarette rests shall be sloped toward the center of the ash receiver. The rests shall be parallel to the outside top edge of the receiver or in each corner, at the manufacturer's option. All surfaces shall be smooth.

[All ashtrays shall be tested accordingly:]

The test shall be made by placing the specimen on its base upon a solid support (a 1¾ inch, 44.5 mm maple plank), placing a steel center punch (point ground to a 60-degree included angle) in contact with the center of the inside surface of the bottom and striking with a hammer in successive blows of increasing severity until breakage occurs. The specimen should break into a small number of irregular-shaped pieces not greater in number than thirty-five, and it must not dice. Any piece ¼ inch (6.4 mm) or more on any three of its adjacent edges (excluding the thickness dimension) shall be included in the number counted. Smaller fragments shall not be counted.

Regulation AA-A-710E

On Zen Koans, New Orleans–Style

Don't believe any false rumors unless you hear them from me.
New Orleans mayor Vic Schiro—his most famous malapropism, which
he said while on TV wearing army fatigues and a battle helmet, check-
ing out damage wrought by Hurricane Betsy